Samuel A. Richmond

Manhood, womanhood

a treatise on secret indulgence and excessive venery : showing how virility is

destroyed, and how restored, with a word of warning to both sexes

Samuel A. Richmond

Manhood, womanhood
*a treatise on secret indulgence and excessive venery : showing how virility is
destroyed, and how restored, with a word of warning to both sexes*

ISBN/EAN: 9783742811424

Manufactured in Europe, USA, Canada, Australia, Japa

Cover: Foto ©Thomas Meinert / pixelio.de

Manufactured and distributed by brebook publishing software
(www.brebook.com)

Samuel A. Richmond

Manhood, womanhood

Yours Truly
S. A. Richmond M.D.
St. Joseph, Mo.

Discoverer of the Samaritan Nervine, and
Author of this, and many other Medical Works.

MANHOOD—WOMANHOOD.

A TREATISE ON

SECRET INDULGENCE

AND

EXCESSIVE VENERY,

SHOWING HOW VIRILITY IS DESTROYED, AND HOW
RESTORED.

WITH A

WORD OF WARNING TO BOTH SEXES.

*Happy is the man that findeth wisdom, and the man that
getteth understanding.*—PROVERBS.

PRICE, - - - $1.50.

PUBLISHED BY
THE DR. S. A. RICHMOND NERVINE CO.,
ST. JOSEPH, MO.
1885.

NOTICE.

In the composition of this work so many authorities have been consulted that it would be almost an endless task to give to each its individual credit, and would have necessitated a constant succession of foot-notes, which would merely have deterred without benefiting the reader. Works of every kind, including the ancient medical classics, the best writers of France, Italy, Germany, England and America, have been carefully searched for information, which has been combined with the author's own experience, discoveries and cases, thus making it the most comprehensive treatise on the subject which has ever appeared in this or any other country.

CONTENTS.

PREFACE.

No excuse should be necessary for publishing a work on
the subject to which this volume is devoted when it is
considered what a vast amount of suffering, an ignorance
of the importance of trifling with the very well-spring of
life, cause not only to the immediate victim, but to
offspring to the third and fourth generations. A knowl
edge of the sexual functions and of that branch of hygiene
which has the genital organs for its care are, unfortunately,
rarely considered a necessary part of the education of
youth, and is too slightly dwelt upon even in the education
of medical men.

The evil arising from ignorance on these topics is one
of great magnitude, and thousands upon thousands of
young men and young women lay the foundations of lasting
physical diseases and cruel mental perversion from not
knowing the consequences of habits learned in infancy or
early youth, certainly pleasurable, apparently harmless, and
which no warning voice of wisdom has taught them to
avoid.

Unconscious of his danger, the young man perseveres in
the enervating habit, his health begins to fail, physicians,

mistaking the cause, treat him symptomatically, time aggravates the danger as it strengthens the morbid appetite for secret indulgence, and impotence, insanity, death, winds up the brief tragedy of life almost before the victim of stolen pleasure has reached his prime.

It is, especially in this country, too true to need repetition that the age of puberty has generally passed before the subject of this book is even alluded to by parent or guardian even in the most casual manner, and then, in all probability, the habit has been acquired and the seeds of future disease are sown.

When one physician alone states that in his own practice in the space of five years, and in a town of not more than 75,000 inhabitants, he has met with one hundred and fifty cases of masturbation leading to involuntary emissions sufficiently grave to utterly ruin the health, and in many of the cases cause death, it will be seen of what importance is the subject on which this work treats. To call the attention of medical men to this source of disease, as well as to point out the great dangers of the fatal habit to such as are not in the profession, is the object of the work. If it is successful in leading the steps of the erring from the precipice they are approaching its end will have been answered.

It is useless in medical men to trifle with this fruitful cause of disease, mental affections, barrenness, impotence, and feeble offspring, when we see all around us, all the time, so many victims of involuntary seminal loss. How difficult it is to treat, and how deplorable the effects arising from its neglect. With the exception of a report of a series of lectures delivered by Dr. Joseph W. Howe, in 1883, in the Medical Department of the University of New York, we have, in this country, no modern work of any high authority on the subject, and, of course, that report is not calculated for the perusal of non-medical readers.

In this work I have culled from every available source, English, French, Italian, the Ancients, and our own authorities, such facts and arguments as have suited my purpose, and in commingling them with the results of my own extended experience, have, I trust, succeeded in producing the most exhaustive work which has ever been published in a popular form, for the non-medical as well as the medical reader.

I have endeavored to give the history of the vice, to point out its dangers, to enumerate the diseases arising therefrom, to instruct parents and guardians as to the signs by which they may know of its existence, to warn the practicers of the degrading and debilitating habit, to give plain directions for its treatment, and serious warning against its continuance.

An old French proverb says : " You cannot make an omelette without cracking eggs," and I have, all through the work, felt the truthfulness of the adage ; but in treating of so delicate a subject, I have done all I could to treat it in a moral and delicate manner, and feel assured that nothing appears in these pages which might cause the judicious to grieve, although hints and innuendos are no more able to stop this terrible scourge of modern society than would teaspoons serve as vessels for the emptying of the Missouri. *Præmonitus præmunitus,* and if, after reading this book, any young man or woman gives way to this body and soul destroying vice of onanism, neither can say that its evils were not sufficiently exhibited, and the consequences pointed out.

The only possible objection to this work which could be raised, is, that such subjects should be for medical men only. If medical men only were addicted to the vice, in this opinion I should agree ; but I have, during a long practice, been painfully impressed with the conviction that the evil is more widely spread than doctors themselves conceive, and strictly medical works do not meet the eye of a great majority of the sufferers.

One English medical man says, in a review of a work on this subject : " It is not very consistent with our national character to dilate so freely on a subject which, in the great majority of cases, can be treated of only as the effects of a most degrading vice." Unfortunately, neither the national character nor the degrading character of the vice prevent its alarming presence amongst us, and I have but little estimation for the character of a physician who would relieve himself from the investigation of a most afflicting and alarmingly common disease, because the subject treated of is an unpleasant and unpopular one.

My firm belief is, that if the medical man, the parent, the guardian, and the pubescent youth, would all post themselves thoroughly on the matter contained in this work it would reduce the number of our sick in a wonderful degree; at any rate, we should not see so many cripples on our streets, consumptives in our hospitals, nor maniacs in our asylums. Certain classes of disease would disappear altogether, and the general condition of humanity would be vastly ameliorated.

With these few words I submit my book to all candid readers.

S. A. RICHMOND.

St. Joseph, Mo., June 21st, 1885.

INTRODUCTION.

A worm is at the root of youth
 Destroying Beauty's bloom,
Devouring, with its canker-tooth,
 And giving to the tomb

Our brightest, best and dearest sons,
 By secret, sure decay ;
Happy the one who wisely shuns
 The vices of the day.

No eyes may see the secret joy,
 Alluring, leading on
The scarcely yet pubescent boy,
 Until his manhood's gone.

His pallid face, his hollow eye,
 His shrinking members tell
The tale of solitary joy
 He learns and knows too well.

Hold your rash hand, misguided youth,
 Cease thus to waste your seed,
You know not half the horrid truth
 Which secret vices breed.

For you no woman's charm shall glow,
 No childish arms embrace,
But manhood's pride shall from thee flow
 And impotence disgrace.

Be warn'd in time! read, mark and learn ;
Ours is a friendly voice.
That you may from self-ruin turn
In manhood to rejoice.

Parents, teachers, ministers, moralists, fanatics, and fools
all combine in keeping from boys, entering on the estate of
manhood, a knowledge of the evils arising from solitary indulgence, perhaps afraid that warning against the evil should
teach the practice. But are they not aware the devil of self-
abuse goeth about like a roaring lion, seeking whom it may
destroy, that, in all probability, the boy has already learned
the insidious and deadly habit from some of his companions,
and that its practice is even now undermining his health,
weakening his reason and, perhaps, unfitting him for the
pleasures and duties of manhood. Gentle mothers, who have
watched with maternal fondness the cradle of your boy's
infancy, would you have the flower blighted just as it begins
to bloom? Fathers, proud of your offspring, the fruit of
your manly vigor, would you see the flower of beauty blasted
in the bud and a secret vice in your son prevent the perpetu-
ation of your name and lineage? It is taking place every day,
and those who fear to speak of such things, who forbid books
treating, in a proper spirit, of such vices being put into the
hands of young people are largely to blame. Children sin
through ignorance, led on by the pleasurable sensations of
the moment, and without any warning voice to cry desist.
Should this be? A thousand times no! It is as absolutely
necessary that boys arriving at puberty should know the evils
arising from solitary vice as it is that chemists should know
the difference between poisons and healthy drugs. But while

these things should be put *plainly* before them they should also be put *purely*, and in the following pages it has been our strongest desire to teach a salutary lesson without arousing dormant passions. We describe the evil to prevent, not to encourage it, and in the portions of it taken from foreign authorities we have selected none but standard authors who have been among the leading medical men of France and England, and who have made the evils of masturbation and sexual excess life-long studies. We have avoided, as much as possible, all medical terms and refrained from loading our pages with treatment, which self-applied is worse than useless. Diseases arising from seminal loss are so obscure in their form, so difficult in diagnosis, and the methods of proper treatment so varied, that it would be worse than useless to lay down general treatment, while the danger is so momentous that any youth or adult suffering from, they know not what, but feeling that something is wrong, should at once consult a physician who has for years made these maladies his special study.

This book should be in the hands of every parent and of every youth in the United States, and the advantages to be derived from its perusal cannot be overestimated.

Yours Truly
S. A. Richmond, M.D.
St. Joseph, Mo.

MANHOOD—WOMANHOOD.

CHAPTER I.

PRECURSORY.

Involuntary emissions of seed present themselves under many aspects and have different degrees of importance only to be judged of by an experienced physician who has made such studies a specialty.

Those which take place spontaneously during sleep, in a chaste and robust individual, may occasionally prove useful in relieving the system of an accumulated excitant, without doing lasting injury to the procreative function. But they are liable to become excessive and dangerous according to their frequency and the constitution of the subject.

These nocturnal emissions are usually, however, produced by an exaggerated excitation of the genitals, due either to excessive coition or to masturbation. An irritating condition remains in the spermatic organs after the termination of the act, whether it be with a female or self pollution, which leads to a secretion of more than the ordinary quantity of semen, which provokes involuntary emissions, under the influence of imperfect erections, and almost without pleasure. At length the relaxation of the ejaculatory passages is such as to lead to the expulsion of the seed without the least erection, or the slightest gratification of desire, and which takes place at stool or the voiding of the urine.

The transition from one class of emission to the other is sometimes so gradual and insensible that neither the sufferer nor the average physician is able to determine when the latter commences. All excessive emissions, in whatever manner made, are equally dangerous, and it is an error to treat seminal losses as separated either in theory or practice.

I retain the names diurnal and nocturnal pollutions, although the seminal loss usually takes place in the night, without erection, without pleasure, it may be occasioned after sunrise by lascivious dreams. But while retaining these names I shall call all abundant seminal evacuations, wherever and whenever they occur, spermatorrhea.

Daily pollutions are not always, as is generally supposed, the result of vicious habits or venereal excesses. Many other causes may occasion them and these influences may be isolated, successive or simultaneous. One thing is certain, whenever they occur, a physician who has made such diseases his special study should at once be consulted.

Among the causes, in addition to those already enumerated, are those which are usually ignored, and which yet are precisely the most dangerous, because their influence is most difficulty to determine, and that they frequently exist without the victim being aware of the fact, until they have made such inroads upon the constitution as to be either totally or almost incurable.

The particular state of the genital organs, and the constitution of the patient require the most careful consideration, and it is the cause of very frequent and serious mistakes that medical men too often assign symptoms to the wrong cause and in consequence pursue a false and fatal treatment.

With the exception of students, who have made this class of

disorder their special study, the history is so little known that it is only by treating each case as a new discovery that the specialist is enabled to restore the sufferer to perfect health.

In the following work I propose to examine the genital organs from every point, gliding rapidly over what is generally known, and endeavoring to clear up all that is obscure and strange. I shall also make liberal use of the recorded cases, numbering some thousands, which I possess, which will best illustrate the most important features and serve to instruct the non medical readers of this work.

CHAPTER II.

INFLAMMATION OF THE SPERMATIC ORGANS.

The most frequent, the most direct and the most energetic cause of nocturnal polution is the inflammation of those organs which are destined to the secretion and excretion of the semen. When the consecutive influence of these inflammations leads to diurnal, or frequent nocturnal emissions, if not checked by proper and vigorous treatment, they will certainly cause insanity and death. The epoch of their appearance is usually unknown, the symptoms are insidious, and their cause very frequently not even suspected. The earliest suspicion however should never be neglected, but once to feel a fear should lead the sufferer to a physician who has made such diseases his special forte. The examinination of such cases calls for the greatest care, patience and experience, as will be seen by the

following case, which I give pretty fully, that the reader may
see how closely and carefully these matters must be attended
to, if any good results are to be hoped for.

Fig. 1.   *Fl. 2*

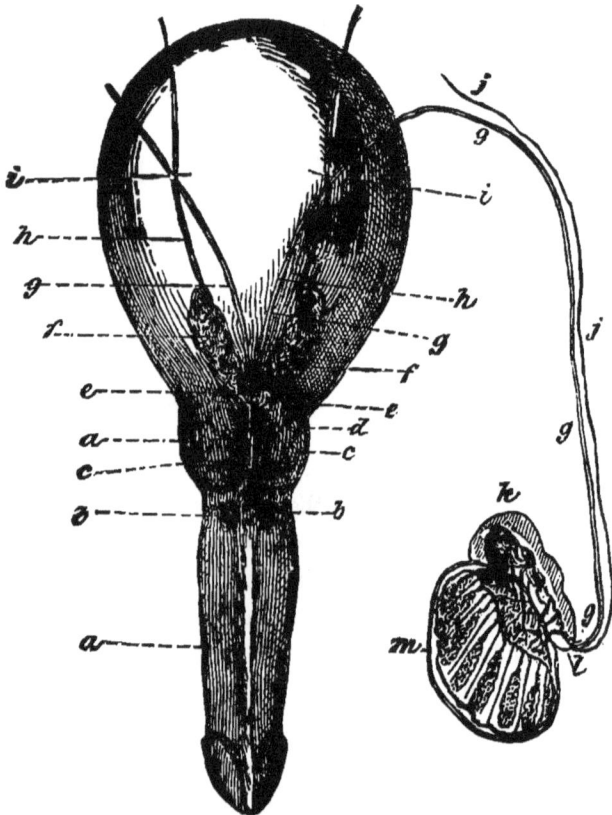

Mr. S., the son of thoroughly healthy parents, himself
robust and of an ardent imagination, received a careful education, and when man-grown devoted himself with affection to

literary pursuits, but was obliged to relinquish his favorite studies for a commercial life. By degrees he became morose and sad, without any known cause, which settled into a profound melancholy. About this period he married, and shortly after when sitting down to write a simple business letter, he was seized with a giddiness and could not conclude it. Of course his family were alarmed and several doctors were consulted, who all had a different cause and a different remedy, which, so far from either naming the disease or providing a cure, left him open to recurring attacks which lasted until the case became desperate and I was called in.

I carefully examined the patient and at once came to my conclusions, requested his wife to reserve some of his urine, which, on examining next day, I found clouded and faintly malodorous, and holding in suspension a glairy substance similar to the white of egg. From these and other symptoms I felt assured that there was not alone a seminal waste but also a chronic inflammation of the prostrate gland and incipient signs of renal suppuration.

Upon making known to the wife the result of my diagnosis she was much surprised, as she had always thought him naturally frigid, that he had never indulged in any excesses at home, and she certainly had no reason to suspect conjugal infidelity; actual coition had always been so rapid, and she had taken so small a share in its consummation that she wondered when she found herself about to become a mother. Little by little, marital embraces became less frequent, and had entirely ceased for over two years. These confidences the more confirmed me in my opinion but the history of the case was still incomplete.

In a favorable moment, when the mind of my patient was

somewhat tranquil, I succeeded in obtaining from him some facts which had never before been made known. When at college he, I found, had been intimate with a domestic in a neighboring farm house, which intimacy was followed by a discharge. This he had carefully concealed, and as he thought cured, with the aid of a friendly drug store clerk. The following year, however, the discharge reappeared, and was arrested by the use of astringents. A slight excess in the drinking of beer during the summer heats however brought it on again, and from that time he had felt but little inclination for female society, and cared nothing for sexual intercourse.

Fully convinced by their confidences I explained to Mr. S. the nature of his malady. He evidently thought me mistaken but promised to watch closely for the signs I indicated. The next day he told me that the last drops of urine were viscous, and that when at stool he had received in the palm of his hand a quantity of similar matter discharged at the same time as the fecal matter. I at once set about the cure and, although it was almost a hopeless case, I succeeded in so building up his vigor that he became quite capable of conducting his business and is the father of two healthy children, besides the sickly one which was born at an earlier date, and which died in its infancy.

Another case which I shall use in illustration before proceeding more fully to explain the symptoms causes and cure was that of Mr. A. P., whose employment was that of clerk on a Missouri steamboat, and who came to me about a year ago, to be cured of a venereal affection which he had contracted, as he said, some three months before, and which had, by some doctor, apparently been cured in a few days.

I could find no external signs of the disease, but the patient complained of violent pains in the head, an aching sensation in the bones, frequent tremblings in the limbs, and continual nervousness. He heard a singing in his ears, felt unpleasant flutterings of the heart, had a dry skin ; his eyes were red, and easily affected by a strong light, etc.

Among all these symptoms there was but one, the bone aching, which pointed to a venereal origin; he also said he suffered more during the night, but his replies to my questions were obscure and frequently contradictory. His constitution seemed fairly robust; his statements led me to suspect his story and fancy him more a hypochondriac than a venereal patient; but it was very evident that there was some derangement of the procreative organs, as he urinated very frequently and with difficulty, complained of severe pain in the member and a throbbing of the testicles. Having noticed these symptoms as general with the victims of nocturnal pollution, I questioned him more closely, but he affirmed he never noticed anything like an escape of semen either when urinating or at stool. That he had only had connection with the woman who gave him the disease, and with her but three times in eight days, I then charged him with masturbation, which, at first, he denied, but at length broke down under my questions and admitted that he had abandoned himself to the habit from the age of ten years, going frequently to the extent of five or six orgasms within the twenty-four hours. He then experienced a tickling sensation, very lively, but unaccompanied by any emission, and terminating in a dull, heavy pain; when about twelve years of age, perceiving that these stolen pleasures injured his health, he became more moderate in the indulgence, but at fourteen abandoned himself to them again with a species of madness.

The irritation was frequently, in fact daily, carried on to
a painful degree, the spermatic cords became engorged, a
weakness in the back and limbs followed, with the noise in
the ears and a partial loss of memory. From seventeen to
eighteen he again moderated his indulgences and somewhat
regained his strength, and it was at this period that he, for
the first time, had commerce with a woman. Soon after came
the disease which he had taken for venereal, and which had
been patched up by a doctor ignorant of the peculiar features
of the case. Having at last discovered the true state of affairs,
I put the patient under proper treatment, and though the
case was one which severely taxed my resources, I ultimately

succeeded in effecting a cure, and I more particularly attended
to it from the fact that the excess of masturbation to which
the patient had devoted himself before the age of puberty,
had rendered the case more critical and the cure more prolonged and complex.

CHAPTER III.

FURTHER CASES AND CURES.

The next case to which I wish to call attention was that of
Lieut. F., of the United States Cavalry, a man of vigorous
constitution, twenty-three years of age, who contracted a
gonorrhœa, which, owing to his service on the plains, was
neglected for some three weeks, after which period he commenced self treatment, dosing himself with copaiba to an unusual extent for five days, which certainly arrested the discharge but brought on a constriction and lively irritation at
the neck of the bladder, characterized by a constant desire to
urinate, and a sharp pain in the perineum during the emission of urine. He was now compelled to go into the military
hospital where, in some two months, he was cured of the
original complaint but at the cost of a chronic inflammation
of the urethra, which was speedily followed by symptoms of
constant diurnal pollution. After much suffering he heard
from a comrade of my success in such cases and put himself under my care. The condition I found him in may
be thus described. Notwithstanding a fair outward appearance of vigor, there was a general feeling of lassitude and

feebleness, the skin covered with pimples, habitual headache, impaired digestion, great flatulence, an entire absence of erection, as of all venereal desire, frequent emission of urine, sixteen to twenty times a day and by spasmodic jerks, short and interrupted. The passage of the urine provoked a keen pain in the orifice of the glans penis, a sharp tickling along the channel of the urethra, a slight raising of the member similar to a semi-erection; the last drops were mingled with a thicker liquid, the urine rapidly decomposed giving out a very unpleasant odor, and depositing an abundant sediment; the orifice of the penis was a deep cherry color and showed inflammation. Within twelve days of his coming to me I reduced the number of urinations to four per day, and he was able to resist, for a long period, the contraction of the bladder; the appetite became good, the digestion easy, the natural erections reappeared and, in twenty days the desire to make water occurred but three times in twenty-four hours and without any pain, without tumefaction of the penis, by a full jet ejected forcibly, the erections energetic and lasting, the digestion was perfect and the sleep profound and refreshing.

It may be useful here to insert the following note, in which a patient, who was himself a student of medicine, has described with remarkable clearness the phenomena which he had observed in himself. The patient had had many attacks of gonorrhea; the first was treated with but little care, and its cure was long and difficult. He counts four attacks of the same nature, but he is not able to say whether they are the offshoots of the first or of a disposition to contract this kind of malady. It was in the month of March that he noticed the first appearance of a discharge, analogous to semen, which oozed from the urethra during the efforts made at stool. The patient does not remember whether this evacuation was accompanied by voluptuous sensations, but in the following instances there was certainly no feeling of pleasure. After every hard stool, which provoked a copious discharge, a general debility and feebleness was felt. In taking necessary precautions to moderate the force of expulsion of urine, he has seen the first drops mingled with a whitish substance, similar to liquid starch, which destroyed the transparency of the urine.

The urethral canal was of extraordinary susceptibility, the orifice always red, inflamed and moist; the liquid which accumulated beneath the foreskin glairy and white ; the emission of urine was accompanied by an irritation of the urethral membrane ; at intervals the patient would feel twinges and ticklings, almost voluptuous, at other times lancing pains like the pricking of pins, and these especially when there was any pressure on the virile member. The patient also noticed that his linen was slightly stained of a yellowish hue ; sometimes he would, in the rectum, feel sensations similar to a slight electric shock.

The organs of generation have lost all their energy, excessive debility preventing anything more than incomplete and brief erections, even under circumstances likely to arouse the passions to the utmost.

I know nothing more of this case, but quote it as a rare example of a patient observing so minutely his own condition and so precisely noting it down.

The next important case, offering much which every reader of this treatise should carefully consider, is that of M. H., a shoemaker, aged 29 years, who came to consult me for a chronic gastritis which for over eight months had resisted all treatment. At the first glance I recognized symptoms which were owing to diurnal pollutions, of the existence of which he appeared to be perfectly ignorant. M. II., of a nervous temperament, had, at the age of eleven years, unhappily contracted the habit of self-abuse, and had only for about two years entirely renounced the practice. From twelve to fifteen he gave himself over to the act from five to six times a day, and his madness was even carried so far that, in quitting the arms of a girl with whom he was criminally intimate, he would abandon himself to his secret excess. In addition to these sins against nature, he at various times contracted disease from promiscuous intercourse, all of which, however, were supposed cured, and at the age of twenty-seven he married and gave himself up to a repetition of the venereal act three or four times a day. Very soon, however, his desires becames less ardent, and there was more difficulty in securing a permanent erection, the semen escaping before the orgasm was completed, and frequently during the night without any knowledge on his part. Sleep ceased to refresh him, and he rose in the morning more wearied than when he retired at night. His digestion became impaired, he was troubled with continued flatulence, the desire to make water was frequent and irresistible, the evacuation of the bladder was by a feeble and interrupted stream, the urine irritated the urethra and had a brick-dust sediment, while giving out a fetid odor. Alarmed by these symptoms he sought medical advice, was treated for dyspepsia, but received no benefit, until, by chance meeting with one of my announcements, he called upon me. After a treatment of a few weeks his appetite improved, his sleep became sound and refreshing, there was a cessation of the constipation, a return of the erections, the urine became

clear, and the face took on a healthy tinge. In the third
week, tormented by frequent and energetic erections, he was
tempted to resume those conjugal functions which had been
now suspended for eight months. Happily this disobedience
to my express commands had no bad effect, and the re-establishment of perfect health followed in its ordinary course.

A very peculiar case was that of Mr. G., a real estate agent's
clerk, who some two years ago made his condition known to
me. When about thirteen years old, a precocious young girl
aroused in him premature erections, with which she used to
satisfy her desires until the discovery of seminal emissions
inspired her with fears of the consequences. All that she had
taught him he in turn practiced on her younger sister, and
these precocious raptures naturally led him to the practice of
masturbation, when he found it was impossible otherwise to
satisfy his desires. This practice he carried on until he was
eighteen years of age, when he succeeded in conquering the
scruples of a young woman he loved, only to find that his
agitation made it impossible for him to profit by her conde-
scension. He attributed this catastrophe to the excess of his
passion, but still felt a profound chagrin and a perfect con-
tempt for himself. He was however more fortunate the
following year, with another female, but paid dear for the
excesses to which he that night devoted himself, for the next
day he had a profuse discharge followed by inflammation of
the testicles ; the right one remaining engorged and enlarged
during five or six months. He made water very frequently
and with much scalding, the last drops were thready, glairy
and produced at the mouth of the bladder the sensation of a
heated iron being applied ; all these symptoms were at their
full height when he came to me, but vigorous treatment and

the use of my Samaritan Nervine, soon allayed the intensity of them and in six weeks I bade my patient good bye perfectly cured.

Although the unhappy habit of masturbation is usually an acquired one from an older or more precocious instructor there are cases in which it has been generated by circumstances over which no control could be exercised and has been commenced at an age when even the imitative faculty was not yet aroused. I have read in a celebrated French medical work the history of a case unexampled in its kind and which I shall here introduce, in the following chapter, being in itself interesting and leading to the discovery of a piquant cause of masturbation in early youth.

CHAPTER IV.

AN ONANIST'S CONFESSION.

I was born robust and of healthy parents. At the age of 12 years I contracted *by myself*, and by the merest chance, the fatal habit of onanism; but it was not long before I perceived the pernicious effect it had on my physical and intellectual functions. A young woman charged to take care of me, probably suspected from my appearance what was the matter and by a severe reprimand caused me to desist. Two months after my health was re-established and I remained stout and happy until I was fourteen years of age.

At this time the Contes de La Fontaine fell into my hands, excited my imagination and renewed the unhappy habit which had been in abeyance for three years.

In the following year, I found to my misfortune, in a corner of my father's library, Aretino, Boccaccio, and other works of the same nature, which I devoured in secret. About this time, I contracted an intimacy with a married lady, who, taking advantage of my inexperience, by kisses and lascivious touches, provoked in me the most violent desires, without permitting me to satisfy them.

All these exciting causes so stirred my nervous system that I was not able to look at a woman without palpitations and a trembling in every limb. Until that time I had not had an involuntary evacuation of semen and, notwithstanding all the provocations by which I was surrounded, I preserved sufficient control over myself not to provoke a pleasurable emission except once a week, on Sunday. The irritation I felt in the genitals was so great that I was frequently compelled to plunge my yard into ice cold water, to allay the irritation I felt. I was tall and well developed for my age, my health was robust, only having somewhat lost my ordinary fullness of flesh.

On the 25th of October, 18—, on awaking, I found myself, for the first time, inundated with semen without having had any knowledge of its emission. During the following eight nights these pollutions were repeated many times, which caused me intense anxiety. I got sensibly thinner, my appetite failed me, I renounced all my studies, I became a walking skeleton, but I did not despair, believing that such an accident would work its own cure, but I grievously deceived myself.

A false modesty restrained me from making my condition known to my father, and I thus found myself thrown upon my own resources to do battle against the terrible infliction, but from that moment it became the unique object of my life, of my thoughts. Concentrated in myself, I detached myself from all my surroundings and occupied my ideas with my case and its cause. I imagined at first that I would tie a string round the prepuce, in such a way that my glans penis should not come in contact with the sheets. This, like all the other means I tried appeared to succeed for a short time, but finished by having no effect. Time and time again upon taking the cord off in the morning I found all the space between the prepuce and the glans penis filled with semen. When I thus saw my health, my strength, my life, my happiness, dribbling to the ground, I could not refrain from tears; a cold sweat broke out from head to foot, I longed for death and called upon him with all my heart.

I rummaged the library, not to search for obscene books, I avoided them as I would a pestilence, but for books of medicine which might point out some method of relief. When I went to bed I was surrounded by folios; Hippocrates, Galen, Ambroise, Parc, collections of treatises, &c., and I spent much of the night in reading in these various authors all which appeared to bear in any way on my condition.

During the year 18—, notwithstanding all the means I took to prevent such a result, I never had less than four pollutions a week. Frequently I would have several every night for fourteen or fifteen nights together, after which would come a remission of three days. This state of things caused me the liveliest fears. I dreaded death and became fearfully thin, I had terrible pains in the spinal column; all movements caused suffering, I even thought I could feel my brain rattle in my head and the joints appeared to have sand in the articulations instead of synovia. During the whole of this winter I remained close to the fire, my extremities were always cold and

I was not able to warm them. Desiring to know something of the human organization, that I might understand these medical books, I frequented a butcher's shop to get some idea of the various parts, which led me to the most extravagant ideas. I read all I could find on *Tabes Dorsalis*, and from those works I endeavored to deduce a method of treatment.

Until this period I had slept on a feather bed, this was replaced by a couch of plain boards with merely a blanket and coverlid. I thought that if I could prevent sleeping upon my back it would stop the pollutions. After many fruitless efforts to correct this habit I made a leather girdle, which I bound round my waist before retiring. To the posterior portion of this was fixed a pointed piece of wood sufficiently prominent to force me to rest either on the one or other side.

I also attributed my pollutions to the habit I had of sleeping with the thighs so close together on my privates, that the genitals being thus compressed were not able to develop themselves freely during the erection without being exposed to rubbings. To obviate this inconvenience I fixed my feet with cords to the sides of the bed, my legs were in this way separated, I having only the power to turn to the right or left with the lower limbs extended as on horseback.

My nightshirt having appeared also to cause excitement and lead to involuntary emissions, by getting folded round my penis during sleep, I discarded it and slept quite naked.

That I might have no fear from the contact of the coverlid, I manufactured a sort of cage of willow work which held it suspended over the parts of generation. Believing that if I could frequently interrupt slumber I should avoid pollutions, I put, in place of a pillow, a large piece of rough timber, which made the head rest uneasily and thus interrupted sleep every few minutes.

I persisted in these self-torments for some years because I feared a loss of semen more than all other miseries. I only kept up the activity of my spirits by inventing new methods or perfecting what I had already employed.

For instance, I imagined that if I girdled the prepuce itself with a knot of the hair growing on my privates, so that when my penis commenced an erection it would pull at the hair and, by thus causing pain, awaken me. This plan I tried, but with little advantage, and afterwards replaced it by another. I surrounded my penis with a flat band, which I rolled and fastened tightly from the root to the head so that there were four or five thicknesses of the cloth between it and the exterior body. I also tried, by the employment of these devices, to extinguish the train of ideas to which I attributed my pollutions. Occasionally I succeeded, but at other times they were merely changed in their object without being less lubricious, for women alone were not the objects of my dreams. My imagination sometimes dwelt upon the most disgusting images: they offered suggestions to me from the lascivious positions of dogs, of stallions and mares, which I chanced to see during the day; I even recall that having seen, one day, two flies copulating, this circumstance was reproduced at night, embellished with all the charms of imagination and provoking an abundant evacuation of semen.

Notwithstanding I avoided with the greatest care all books, pictures and images susceptible of calling up erotic ideas, they would arise. I flew from the presence of females, I gave up horseback riding, carriage driving and all heating food and drinks. In the excess of my despair I had recourse to devotion and promised to become converted if I could only obtain a cure.

That which most astonished my family was the change seen in my character; I became gloomy and ill humored; I avoided sunlight and wore my hat over my eyes, for bright daylight made me sick; I spoke little, and notwithstanding my sufferings I never complained.

As nobody suspected the motives which actuated my conduct, I was looked upon as an original, a hypochondriac, a misanthrope, etc. I was indifferent to all the pleasures of my age; I hated society because I could not bear to see the happiness of others in opposition to my own miserable condition; I was, when in it, ill at ease; I was always desiring to change my position; if I was forced to remain it was agony to me, and I longed for the moment when I could regain my solitude.

In 18— the order of my troubles changed but I became no happier; the pain in my loins was altered to severe colics, sharp and of long continuance, coming on after each meal. I had a prodigious appetite, which accorded with the idea that very much food was necessary to replace the seminal losses.

I had read in a medical book that milk, eggs and figs produced large quantities of semen, and I gorged, at every morning meal, eggs, milk and figs. I had read that good wine was a sovereign remedy for weakness, and I daily drank huge draughts of the purest wine I could procure. After every meal I had acidity of the stomach, colics and flatulence; the bowels were blown up as with gas, which again forced me to forego whatever society I might be in.

Throughout the year a constant diarrhœa troubled me, and I frequently spent an hour at stool. Convulsive spasms were felt in the muscles of the thighs, the arms and at the corners of the eyes.

I resolved many times to diet myself or to diminish the quantity of food, but I suffered so much from hunger that I found it impossible to persevere in such a course.

Having read in some book the good effects of cold bathing, I took frequent baths in the Loire; but these, even in the dog days, were followed by chills and colics; an icy coldness made me shiver all the day; my constitution was too feeble to get up a healthy reaction.

Later on, when I went to bed, I fastened my genital organs in a kind of white metal box, fixed round the waist by straps, but while I thus escaped the accidental friction of the penis I found the compression insupportable.

At another time, for the purpose of awakening myself at the moment I should have a lascivious dream, I tied the relax-ed penis close down between the testicles. The pain caused by an erection certainly woke me, but it also forced me to de-tach the ligature, and I was exposed to the same accident; sometimes, even, I felt it come at the moment I loosened the cord: at others the movements necessarily made round the penis in freeing it from its confinement caused an expulsion of semen.

At the same period I found out that the fullness of the bladder in the morning disposed one to a seminal orgasm, and I resolved to abstain from drinking during the day, which thirsty as I always was, was a terrible deprivation. I always made water before getting into bed, and I placed by my side an alarm clock which aroused me at stated times to empty the bladder. These plans were efficacious at first, but soon lost all power.

One day I examined myself in a mirror. My eyes were dry and hollow, my complexion leaden. I could count my ribs and the prominent bones of my skeleton. Almost all my hair fell out, and the portion which remained was so painful to the touch that I fancied I was suffering from *le plique polonaise*.

I then investigated all those parts of my body which were accessible to the sense of smell and found about them a cadaverous odor.

I carefully examined my urine and my excrement. I remarked at the bottom of the chamber vessel a soapy sediment, which I imagined was formed in the bladder, and I fancied myself afflicted with stone, attributing for a long time all my sufferings to this cause, especially the stomach pains and the sharp, piercing ones which sometimes occurred in the canal of the urethra.

I saw in my excrement many little worms. I thought they were of the same kind as those which live on the decayed flesh of the corpse. I myself so much resembled one that their premature presence did not astonish me.

I habitually felt in the rectum lively, creeping pains, which I attributed to these ascarides.

The nostrils were occasionally the seat of similar feelings.

I had continued palpitations, which I attributed to disease of the heart.

Disgusted with life, I sought many times the means of suicide, but always, at the moment I would carry them into effect, the courage so to do so deserted me. Given over to the most frightful despair, not knowing what to do, and seeing the happy condition of the lower classes, I wished to descend to their level, thinking it might ameliorate my condition. I announced to my family that I had a desire to learn the cabinet-maker's art. They consented, for they had become accustomed to what they called my bizzarreries, my low-lived propensities. But the truth was I was constant to nothing on earth, and when I took a fancy in my head no human consideration could make me abandon it.

During the next three months I learned to turn and to handle tools. Soon tired of this kind of life, I became, in turns, carpenter, mason, laborer. I lived like these workmen, I labored as they did, thus hoping to become as robust as they. But I was not long able to sustain such rude living.

The changability of my disposition was a problem with all who surrounded me. If the pollutions ceased for two or three days I became less morose, more sociable. The pollutions recommenced I became as isolated as before. They altered the very character of my voice, taking away its force and vigor. When they ceased it regained its power and I could read aloud in the family circle, but as soon as the pollutions reappeared I was forced to renounce this exercise, to the astonishment of those who had heard me, and whom I was not able to take into my confidence.

In stooping one day to pick something up I felt a crackling sensation in the left ear, followed by a singing, which has never quitted me from that epoch. It was accompanied by pains in the teeth, which were almost continual for two years.

In brief, language fails me to express all the horrors of my situation. Sleep disturbed by horrible dreams failed to refresh. I rose in the morning suffering as though all my limbs had been beaten with rods. Sometimes I felt like remaining in bed, but if I gave way to this deceptive desire I was not slow to repent it. When I have had three or four pollutions the same night, with what anguish I have marked

the approach of day. I have wished myself ten feet under
ground. The terrors of my imagination have caused a cold
perspiration which inundated me, and it was with difficulty
that I made myself free from the cords with which I had
bound myself.

Frequently I have determined to fly altogether from human
society, to hide myself in some obscure retreat, and there
with bitter tears invoke death. If my eyes permitted me to
read, I would carry with me J. J. Rosseau, Young's Night
Thoughts, and Blair's Grave, and, by way of medicine, a
collection of autopsy cases, for which I had a peculiar prede-
liction.

In 18— my pollutions ceased during the winter. I gath-
ered flesh; I came, little by little, more into society, from
which I had been so long estranged. I do not know to what
cause I can attribute this happy change, but it was not of
long duration. At the return of Spring I fell again into my
former condition.

I attributed this fugitive freedom from nocturnal emissions,
which I had enjoyed, to an iron ring fastened by a padlock
and attached by two cords. It had in its upper, inner surface
two sharp points of steel. My penis, when not in a state of
erection, was easily placed in this confinement, but when it
swelled the space became too circumscribed, it pressed strongly
against the points, which caused so severe a pain that I awoke
with a start, I then detached the ring and my pain ceased;
when the erection was over I replaced the ring, and so on
from time to time.

Until this period I had felt no inconvenience in my chest,
but being one day exposed to a rain storm I was seized the
following morning by an intense pleurisy, which was followed

by a stubborn cough accompanied by a debility, which confined me almost constantly to my easy chair. I now thought myself consumptive and hoped soon to be at rest. But I recovered somewhat during the winter of 18—, and my health became again the object of my liveliest solicitude.

In the spring I had, as in the preceding year, a return of the pollutions, which again threw me into the most deplorable condition.

In 18—, seeing that nothing seemed to arrest the seminal discharges, I had the idea of returning to masturbation as a curative process. I had always four or five emissions a week, sometimes eight, and I reasoned to myself, "If am able to rule the course of nature, and replace by other and less frequent means these involuntary emissions, there will be a net. gain in my favor." I recommenced then, by careful calculation the habit from which I had for five years restrained.

This course succeeded very well for about fifteen days, but I was obliged to suspend it, as with all other plans, use destroyed its efficiency. I returned then to my last plan, the iron ring, in which I made some modifications, because the points. placed above had ulcerated the surface of the penis and I was. compelled to change their position.

I tried river bathing a second time, but this did me more harm than before because I had become weaker.

Having exhausted all the resources which my imagination was able to suggest, nothing was left for me but travel. I wished to go to Montpellier because I had heard that the climate was favorable for the weak chested ; my father consented, and the hopes created by the anticipated change gave me sufficient vigor to accomplish the journey on foot.

Before concluding the history I must add that I have been

frequently menaced with attacks of appoplexy, almost to the loss of consciousness, and that leeches applied to the arms or perineum have invariably done more harm than good.

CHAPTER V.

MEDICAL REMARKS ON THE CASE.

The physician to whom he applied at Montpellier makes the following remarks upon this case:

"Shortly after his arrival at Montpellier, M. D. came to consult me, and interested me much with the naive and animated account of all which his memory could recall.

"I believed at first, as he did, that these nocturnal pollutions were the result of an extraordinary sensibility in the genital organs produced by the precocious abuse which he had practiced, but before undertaking the case I got him to write down the memoir printed above, that I might forget nothing, and have the facts presented to me in proper order. Some time after he sent me this narrative illustrated with drawings representing the various machines and methods he had used in the vain efforts to restrain his nocturnal pollutions.

"In thinking the matter over, I was struck by the existence in the fecal discharges of those little worms, which the unfortunate young man regarded as the proof of approaching death. I examined his anus but failed to find there any traces of the ulceration to which he had attributed the pricking, tickling pains which he had experienced in the rectum, and had it been there it would not have accounted for a similar sensation in the nose.

"I then imagined that those nocturnal pollutions might be caused by the presence of ascarides, and I advised him to pay particular attention to this subject. He very soon told me, that he habitually voided these minute worms, that many times, urged by the incessant and powerful tingling, he had forced his finger into the anus, and that on withdrawing it he had found, under his nail, one of these ascarides still living.

"He had, at this time, a very sour mouth, and during the night discharged a great quantity of saliva upon his pillow, etc.

"Having made this careful diagnosis, I treated him in accordance with the opinion formed and very soon found the pollutions cease rapidly and permanently. All the accidents which were the cause of them disappeared, vigor and flesh were regained with remarkable celerity. But it was only by moderate co-habitation with females that he recovered entirely."

This history is a true drama, a drama complete and full of interest, in which is seen an iron necessity pressing incessantly on its unhappy object, who fought with courage and perseverance against ills which he had in no way deserved.

It is absolutely necessary to have passed through such an ordeal; it is imperative to write under the power of such a calamity, and to have in the mind but this one fixed idea to be able to retrace all the circumstances with such truth. The recital of a third party would be impossible to approach it. These details unveil to us, fully, the mysteries of the human heart.

What is there in the lives of these unfortunate invalids

which we so unfittingly blame; when we ought to pity and
above all to cure them? In this case, as in others which have
come under my notice, patients tormented by ascarides have
delivered themselves over to onanism before arriving at puberty; they bitterly accuse themselves, and regard the unhappy
habit as the cause of those pollutions which become a curse.
I would not seek to diminish the just horror which this
deplorable habit ought to inspire, but truth before all things:
these infants, in my opinion, are more unhappy than culpable.
To have such a passion established spontaneously before the
entire development of the genital organs, it is necessary for
the sufferer to become the victim of a pathological irritation.

The presence of a stone in the bladder frequently, with
young boys, causes precocious erections, the pains caused at
the mouth of the urethra they endeavor to allay by rubbing the
end of the penis, and from this cause we usually find in such
cases the foreskin unusually long. These fingerings, generally
conduct them to a habit for which they cannot be morally
responsible.

The action of worms in the rectum provokes the same
phenomena in a way still more constant. I have frequently
seen infants of two or three years tormented by erections
almost permanent, which were due to no other cause. Naturally enough these children carry their hands to the part
which incommodes them and continue to rub the penis, just
as they do the nose when it itches, but the sensation which
results from the rubbing of so sensitive an organ as the penis
is much more lively, and leads them on with a power almost
irresistible. Why must it be a worse crime for these children to rub one member more than another?

When the power of reasoning comes with puberty the victims of these early complaints are, perhaps, able to resist the powerful inclinations, but then they prove by nocturnal pollutions that the same cause which made them onanists is at work, which is the irritation of the genital organs by the worms lodged in the rectum.

These ascarides not infrequently produce similar or analogous effects with the female. I have seen very many girls of tender age who were tormented by irresistible ticklings and tinglings in the genital organs, by abundant leuchorrheas, or whites, accompanied by a redness and excoriation of the clitoris and the inner lips, which evidently arose from the same cause.

These phenomena are constant, general, and, so far as I have observed, common to both sexes.   .

Seminal losses which take place during stool with those who are afflicted by ascarides cannot be ascribed to a compression of the seminal vessels, for there is no constipation. They can only be looked upon as analogous to nocturnal pollutions ; we must then admit that the continued titillation exercised in the rectum and on the margin of the anus by the ascarides extends its influence to the genital organs and produces spasmodic contractions of the seminal vessels.

I have, myself, known many cases where the acquiring of the habit was spontaneous and owing to the trouble caused by worms in the rectum and around the margin of the anus. Among others, that of R., a high-school student in the city in which I have my medical institution. At fifteen years of age he was troubled with frequent and prolonged erections. One night, wishing to allay the intolerable itching at the extremity of his penis, he rolled it rapidly between his two hands, and was surprised at the voluptuous sensation which

this movement provoked ; he repeated it and was not less
astonished at the evacuation which resulted. Some days
after the same causes recalled the remembrance of the sensations and naturally led to the same maneuvres. The practice
was carried on until the habit became a passion, and when I
undertook the case, which I happily cured, he looked like a
youth in the last stage of consumption.

Another of my patients received the first hint that pleasure
was to be procured by friction of the genitals from riding on
horseback, and he could never go beyond a walking pace
without having an erection, and, if the trotting was continued, an emission.

Another case which I have had come within my practice
and occurring with very young children, is that of going to
sleep extended upon the stomach.   During slumber the genitals become heated and the penis erects itself before there are
any signs of puberty ; pressure against the bed provokes titillation, and the rubbings and movements thus excited lead to
abuses as fatal as those of masturbation.   It was in one case,
beyond a doubt, this position alone which provoked the discovery of these fatal pleasures, since the patient was in the
most complete ignorance of everything connected with sexual
matters, and had certainly never had a bad example.   Further,
he was naturally so modest and so reserved that he never
could have permitted or been able to suffer the least manual
interference with his virile member.   The first impression
was ·then purely instinctive and accidental, but it none the
less became the starting point of a habit which became an
irresistible passion without changing its nature.

Another of my patients, of lymphatic temperament and a
very precocious intelligence, was troubled by worms during

the first years of his life. When about eight years of age he slept with his nurse maid and found a pleasure in pressing himself against her bare flesh without knowing why, and gazing at, without making any remarks, those female parts which he had before never seen.   These acted on an ardent imagination and threw him into a kind of melancholy, the true cause of which no one for a moment suspected. When thirteen years of age a young lady of eighteen gratified herself very frequently by arousing his desires, but only permitted him to make movements on the exterior of her person.   Shortly after he went to college where these remembrances followed him and employed his imagination. and at night he imitated his movements with the girl as nearly as possible. He thus contracted a habit fully as fatal as masturbation, though he always abstained from using his hands. The most painful feature of this case when it first came under my notice, was the libertinage of the ideas contrasted with the absolute incompetence of the agents of execution ; the genitals were very little developed, the penis wrinkled and short, the prepuce very long and the testicles small.

The first and most important of all the causes capable of provoking the abuse of the organs of generation is the peculiar organization of the man.

With the greater number of animals, the male is not excited to copulation except by the presence of the female, and then only when she is in the necessary condition for fecundation ; this moment passed and they live together as if they were of the same sex. It is, ordinarily, the odor emanating from the sexual organs of the female during heat which arouses the sexual feelings of the male ; but whatever may be the cause the action is but little prolonged, and when over they return to the most complete indifference. How widely different is the condition of mankind. As soon as the testicles acquire their full development until they shrivel and wither from age the secretion of sperm is always taking place. It may be augmented or diminished by exciting the organs, but it is never entirely suspended while the tissues preserve their integrity. This well known and highly important fact has been too much neglected ; it is easy to derive from it a useful application. The configuration of the superior members must also exercise a great influence on the passions of human nature. Many animals are able to indulge in copulation at all seasons of the year ; their seed is always ripe for fecundation · it

always contains the spermatazora ; among them the cock and
the pigeon have a greater faculty for copulation than a man,
but it is impossible for them to provoke an evacuation of
semen without the assistance of the female. The most prolonged deprivation of sexual opportunity of birds has never
been followed by any any act resembling masturbation. It is
true that birds of diffelent species will couple if their own
kind be not available, but even such lapses are extremely rare.

Many of the mammalia have testicles and erectile tissues
more voluminous than those of mankind, and exhibit, during
the rutting season, a prolific power far superior to ours.
They are more energetically solicited to copulation, and accept
the invitation with audacity. Notwithstanding this high degree of erotic ardor, they do not ordinarily annoy the female
which refuses them, but merely the one as eager for the fray
as themselves.

I have seen a male ass, when not employed in the getting
of mules, place his forefeet on his manger and then bring
forward the hinder members until the penis was embraced,
when violent efforts to accomplish the venereal act were
attempted. Every one has remarked the abundant emissions
of sperm which stallions and jacks after having been long
kept in a state of erection by the neighborhood of a female
in heat.

A menagerie elephant, since deceased, procured for himself frequent and abundant ejaculations by the assistance of
certain movements which he had learned, and his death was
attributed to this cause.

The bear's conformation approaches somewhat to that of
man; and frequently during the rutting season, those in the
Jardin des Plantes have been noticed carrying their paws

violently to their genitals, abandoning them after rapid movements, and shortly returning to the same movements. If
these efforts are not successful, it is not the inclination
which is wanting. I have seen one of the largest male bears,
in one of those moments of erotic madness, extended as in
the act of copulation, with the belly on a rock. After rapidly
moving backward and forward for some time, all motion
would suddenly cease, and a total state of exhaustion would
follow.

Finally, the monkey, of all the animal tribe, more nearly
in conformation approaches man, and it is well known with
what rage monkeys will give themselves up to masturbation.

To the physiological dispositions, more pronounced with
man than any other animal, must be added many accidental
influences, pathologically caused. I have already spoken of
ascarides, the erections they provoke, and the evil habits
which follow and cutaneous affections attacking the penis.

CHAPTER VI.

THE DANGERS SURROUNDING YOUTH.

There seems to be a close sympathy between the organs of
generation and widely separated maladies, which it is hard to
explain. Dr. Desportes has pointed out a species of *angina*,
which is frequently preceded by a grand developement of the
venereal passion, and a disposition to all kinds of abuse.

Pulmonary complaints frequently coincide with great lubri-
city. Many practitioners have thought that such disorders

have been excited by such, and which have arisen from the
effect on the genitals, but in my opinion it is the sexual abuse
which has caused the pulmonary trouble.

Others have believed that masturbation is able to produce
priapism and satyriasis, but it is evident they have taken the
cause for the effect. All genital abuses produce an entirely
opposite result; and it is easily understood that priapism and
satyriasis, from whatever cause, cannot endure for any length
of time without provoking handling of the organs, and the
result is easily seen.

We must, then, freely concede that man carries in his
nature the first germs of his errors.

I should be very sorry to diminish, in any degree, the just
sentiment of aversion which these vices inspire,—a feeling
which society must carefully cherish for its own preservation.
But justice will not permit me to confound the unfortunate
with the criminal. Truth is above all; it is always useful;
and to be able to use it we must look at it squarely in the face.
It is the not having understood it, which has created institutions incompatible with human nature, and fallen into exag-
gerations of which I intend to point out the danger, not only
to the individual but to social order.

In all I shall say on this sad subject, I shall expose as
clearly as possible, and without either exaggeration or after-
thought what I have observed during a long practice, beginning with the exterior causes acting on children before
arriving at the age of puberty.

The most attentive and clear-sighted parents believe themselves exonerated from watching the actions of their children
in relation to their genital organs, until they are compelled by
signs of approaching evolution ; in the same manner medical

men are disposed to neglect any mention of bad habits until the same period. These are errors to be guarded against, for there are many causes in operation which may lead to abuse from the earliest period,—the cradle and the nursery are not exempt.

An unhappy infant yet at the nurse's breast may be made the victim of her stupidity. She will remark that playing with the little one's genital organs will calm its cries and promote sleep more readily than any other course ; she repeats the operation with variations, without noticing that repose is preceded by spasmodic movements ; they augment ; they take on a convulsive character ; the infant sinks rapidly and becomes more difficult to calm. At first I may suspect worms, teething, &c., but having observed certain gestures, I examine the genital parts and find the penis in a state of erection. I understand it all now. Of course the nurse thinks that at this age she is able to tickle these parts as she would the chin. She must be dismissed, for her presence is enough to recall sensations to the infant to whom she has taught the habit of expecting them. Time and strict attention are necessary to entirely remove the impressions ; with these, the re-establishment of health is an easy matter.

Later, male children are exposed to the same dangers from the maids who have charge of them, and it is not ignorance alone which can be laid to their charge. These are the girls who, carried away by the ardor of their temperament, and dreading the result of more serious connections, do not hesitate to corrupt to their own sensual pleasure the little boys under their charge, even in their earliest infancy. It is thus that many patients have been corrupted at ages varying from five to eight years. Even if these premature pleasures stop by chance, or by a fortunate discovery, they leave in the sexual organs a precocious excitability, which is liable to provoke self-abuse, and their entire future existence is compromised. That which Rabelais recounts of the early education of Gargantua, the pleasantness of his maids, their caresses, &c., is not a picture under which is hidden some severer truth, but, unhappily, the expression, a little crude but faithful, of that which too frequently happens to children, blindly abandoned to the care of hireling hands.

Of course these dangers are augmented as the organs become developed. Examples of this kind are too numerous to need citation, and it is no matter of astonishment when we know that these servant girls live in a state of celibacy, that they are highly fed and lightly worked, and that to become pregnant would ruin them for life, while generally a neglected education prevents them dwelling on moral turpitude.

What is still more difficult to conceive is that many boys are perverted by men servants and male preceptors. I am not alone in this opinion ; all physicians who have written on the subject allude to it. One of my patients was initiated into the habit by a young girl of eighteen, who had made the boy an instrument of her erotic desires. Others have been seduced into masturbation by the wanton games of mature ladies, widows, and wives whose husbands were away, long before puberty had rendered them able effectually to copulate.

There is another very fruitful cause of disorder, more common, though much less known. I mean the precocity of certain children under the influences of ideas produced from gazing on female nudity.

The desire to pry into the secrets of woman are generally developed at the same time as the organs of generation, and it is generally therefore supposed that all the curiosity and desire find in this the starting point. But it frequently happens that the genital instinct manifests itself before puberty, and even in the most tender infancy.

A close observation of children will assure us that long before the descending of the testicles an instinctive attachment draws boys to the other sex, and that an inquiet curiosity is aroused. It is very evident that they treat a girl very different from a boy ; that they seek in her the attributes of her sex, although they have no very clear idea as to what they are. This is the mystery which occupies their thoughts, the solution of which torments them without ceasing. They are seen continually peeping about the maids, their sisters, all who wear a petticoat. We usually laugh at these infantile

tricks, but if we watch them more seriously we shall find by
no equivocal signs that the genital instinct is aroused. We
see a boy stealthily creep behind a girl who goes into a retired
spot for a private purpose, another will sit under a ladder
upon which a girl is mounted, remain hidden under a balcony
to see the legs of a woman who may be on it, steal furtively
into the bed-room to assist at the toilet of a sister, or to gaze
on her exposed breasts and limbs while she is sleeping. They
do not know what they are looking for, but a secret impulse
urges them on, awakens and guides their intelligence, and
usually finishes by finding out something. Their ideas are
vague, but their sensations are lively, and leave in their young
imaginations a profound impression, the memory of which
will remain clearly fixed at ripe age, and even during the
whole of a long life.

I have been able to judge of the power of these souvenirs
and the ravages they have made by the minute details entered
into by some of my patients, on circumstances of this nature
which had taken place thirty or forty years before, and which
had a baleful influence on their whole future life.

One of them came very near drowning at six years old from
contemplating, with too much affection, the naked legs of a
young washerwoman.   He was getting nearer to the river
bank to see these limbs more clearly, when the ground gave
way, and he would have been drowned if the woman he had
watched had not come to his assistance.   He was forty-five
when he gave me these details, his health was ruined by diurnal pollutions arising from masturbation, and the memory of
those naked legs contributed all those years to work his
imagination into an erotic fury.

Another, at the age of seven, was taken with his mother

and some female friends on a bathing excursion in a pleasant river. Notwithstanding their bathing suits and all the care they took, he remarked the difference in form from men, and when seated on the knees of one of these ladies he felt an indescribable pleasure in pressing his hand against the protruberance he had remarked and whose firmness and roundness he appreciated with a lively sensation of delight. The sensations he felt were so strongly shown and by such evident signs that it was judged advisable to prevent further observations; but those he had made never left his memory. His imagination gloated over them afterwards until solitary pleasures were attempted and their success ruined his health.

Others have surprised a woman sleeping in an exposed position, or have gazed on the naked breasts of a nurse or a cookmaid, and these apparitions, seemingly so harmless, have been the subject of endless conjectures, until some other chance has led to the discovery of prurient pleasures, which were augmented by dreaming on what they had seen. But let us hear what Rosseau has said on the subject in the first book of his "Confessions."

"As Mlle. Lambercier had for us the affection of a mother, so also she had a mother's authority, and sometimes carried it to the length of infantile chastisement when we deserved it. She threatened me for a long time and the threat appeared very terrible, but after its execution I did not find the punishment so bad as the fear of it had been ; and what is stranger still, the punishment made me more in love than ever with her who had inflicted it, and all my love for her, all my natural sweetness of disposition, could not restrain me from seeking for further examples of the chastisement by deserving it, for I had found in the pain, and even in the shame, a melange of sensuality which had left more desire than fear of being again so used by the same plump white hand. It is true, without doubt, that the feeling was mingled with some precocious idea of sex, as the same punishment from the hand of her brother was not at all pleasant. The second time she applied the punishment was also the last, for she doubtless perceived by some sign that this chastisement did not answer its intended purpose, and she declared that she would renounce it, and I, by an accident which I could not help, deprived myself of the honor of being treated by her as a little boy.

"Who would believe that this punishment of infancy, received at eight years from the hands of a woman of thirty, has decided all my tastes, all my desires, all my passions for the rest of my life? Tormented for a long time without knowing by what, I devoured with an ardent eye all the beautiful female forms, my imagination recalling them without cessation, only to put them to work in the same way, and make them do with me as had been done by Mlle. Lambercier.

"Even after arriving at full puberty, this strange taste was always persistent and was carried almost to depravity, almost to a mania. * * * * *

"My old infant taste, in place of vanishing, associated itself so closely with the maturer one that I was never able to separate desires called up by my senses; and this folly joined to natural timidity has always rendered me but little enterprising among women, fearing to say all or have all my wishes fulfilled, the kind of enjoyment of which the other was but the last term was not unsurped by that of sexual desire, and she who was able to accord it. I have thus passed my life in longing for, and remaining silent in the presence of the women

I most loved and most desired. Not daring to declare my taste, I amused it at any rate by the recollection which preserved the idea. It may be conceived that this method of love-making did not secure rapid progress, and was not very dangerous to those who were the subject of it. I have possessed very few but I have not failed to enjoy very many after my manner —that is to say by the imagination.

"It may be imagined what such an avowal as this has cost me, or that which throughout the course of the course of my whole life, carried sometimes near to those I loved by the fury of a passion which took away the power of vision, of hearing, of understanding, and seized by a convulsive trembling in all my body which :prevented me from declaring to them my folly and imploring of them in the most intimate familiarity the only favor which outweighed all others, that which only happened once and that in my infancy.

" I had with a little Miss Goton some tete-a-tetes sufficiently short, but sufficiently lively, in which she condescended to play schoolmistress, and that was all ; but this all, which, in effect, was all for me, appeared in my eyes the supreme of happiness. * * * * * * "

I have thus quoted Rosseau at some length, because no author has better rendered similar details, and because they illustrate perfectly the tenacity of early impressions. In reading what the same writer says in his third book "*of that dangerous supplement which deceives nature, which permits us to dispense with all the opposite sex without feeling the want of its assistance,*" we see how these remembrances have been able to represent themselves to his memory in his solitary moments, that he had not been able at thirty years to conquer them, and never speaks of them without emotion." And it is thus that we can understand "that the infantile chastisement had decided all his tastes, all his desires, and all his passions for the balance of his life."

I have under my eyes a mass of confessions of the same character, which would merit the same publicity if they were written with the same elegance. There is, however, one case which I will report in all its details.

CHAPTER VII.

A SERIES OF SINGULAR CASES AND REMARKS.

M. D., the son of a distinguished medical man, when about six years old, was, one hot summer day, with a maid servant of the house, who believed that she might act with perfect freedom in the presence of a child of that age, so she stripped herself and extended herself upon a couch in a complete state of nudity. But the little D. had followed every movement, had studied every difference of form with avidity, and crept close to her, as though he would also enjoy an afternoon's nap, but he became so bold in his actions, so suggestive in his gestures that, after having laughed at him for some time, she was compelled to put him out of the room. This young girl had been merely imprudent, and the circumstance only occurred once, but the boy profoundly guarded the remembrance of all which he had seen to such a degree that, when he consulted me, forty years afterwards he had not forgotten the most trifling circumstance of that early initiation into the mysteries of the female form.

The continued preoccupation of mind by these images produced no immediate effects, but at eight years old the most insignificant accident caused him to turn his souvenirs to his ruin. Being mounted on one of those old-fashioned clothes horses which served for brushing wardrobes, he had slid down the transverse bar, and the rubbing of the genitals by this movement proved so pleasant that he hastened to remount in the same place and repeat the motion which had given him so much enjoyment. Repetition and a varying of the movements procured for him sensations to which his young mind had hitherto been a stranger. This fatal discovery, combined with the recollections which ruled his entire being, led to abuse the most strange that could be conceived, and later on to masturbation the most inveterate.

I need not follow all the recital of the miseries which were the consequence of this unhappy passion. Let it suffice to make known the extraordinary means which he was obliged to take to restrain himself from indulging in the overwhelming propensity.

He slept on the hardest of beds, without his shirt so as to avoid all friction, covered with a single sheet sustained by a hooped canopy ; having the arms elevated and crossed under his head ; a domestic passed the night watching to arouse him if he once changed his position. When he arose he put next his skin a coat of mail weighing twenty-two pounds, similar to those worn by ancient warriors, with the exception of having no sleeves. Below it was armed with a silver basin destined to receive the genital organs ; the suit of mail was provided with four openings, two for the arms and two for the thighs. This coat of mail was so hinged as to open in front to admit the body ; after it was closed it was laced by a

chain of metal, a padlock being passed through the last link
of the chain, the key of which was given in charge to a faithful domestic, charged with the strictest orders not to give it
to the wearer on any pretext. Guarded by the silver basin
the genitals were completely isolated, only a small aperture
existing in the lower part for the escape of the urine. For
further precaution, the patient had four needles soldered on
the upper part of the interior of the median line so as to
directly oppose all erection.

He had worked industriously to so perfect this suit that it
would not permit him to make the slightest infraction, and
for nine or ten months he had not dared to dispense with it,
notwithstanding the frequent inflammations caused by the
friction of the basin which occurred on the testicles and
adjoining parts. Many times he had attempted to pick the
lock, after in vain soliciting the key from its keeper. He
frequently, like a madman, beat upon the metallic barrier,
which withstood all his efforts. Notwithstanding all these
precautions, his moral and physical condition was in a deplorable state, which caused me to suspect daily pollutions. But
how was proof of this to be ascertained? How was treatment
to be carried on without suspending the means of repression?

I ought to remark that in all cases where I shall speak of
infants of five or six years, who have not given signs of
puberty until many years afterwards, and who have not been
directly initiated into the vice of onanism by any one, it will
be to prove that the sexual ideas are spontaneously developed
years before the evolution of the genital organs.

I shall also show further on that the same precocity is
noted with a great number of infants of the other sex. At
present I will content myself by quoting an observation of

Dr. Parent-du-Chatelet, remarkable in many points : He speaks of a little girl who, from the age of *four* years, gave herself up to the greatest irregularities with little boys from ten to twelve years of age. She had, notwithstanding, been raised with a grandmother, a woman of high respectability and marked piety. I suppress here the details which were made during a legal inquiry. I have alone wished to point out that this little girl was in the best condition to escape from such peculiar passions, yet she debauched boys who had two or three times her own years, and these things went on daily during four years without anything arising which, from childish indiscretion, might have made the facts suspected.

An important scientific fact arises from these details, which is that with a great number of infants the sexual instinct manifests itself with enormous force many years before the evolution of the genitals has commenced.

From this fact the practical conclusion may be drawn that it is not sufficient to await the approach of puberty before exercising the greatest care to remove from infantile attention immodest things, and to avoid arousing their curiosity on sexual matters.

Very many parents, in this respect, are inconceivably short-sighted ; they allow children of both sexes to play together for entire hours without the least superintendence, as though nothing wrong could occur. In this crowd of children it would not be difficult to find one more fully instructed than the others, and even supposing that none have questions to ask or revelations to make, it would be wonderful if they played together very long in full liberty without one or other making some discovery, and then you may imagine how the new found excitement will spread with the rapidity of light-

ning and the most impenetrable secrecy. The confidence of
many parents in the ignorance of their children, permits
them to indulge in other imprudent acts in their presence,
such as the evidences of amorous affection which they
exchange before them. Frequently the same chamber, the
same alcove contains the beds of the one and the other. It
is not always in the power of parents to remedy this inconvenience, but all must not be persuaded that childish sleep is
as real as it pretends to be.

It is sufficient to merely indicate these facts and allow each
one to draw his or her own conclusions, so I will now enter
on a question of which the weight is felt by all who have
written on masturbation—I mean the influence of places of
public and private education. If I am allowed to judge by
my own observation, of *ten* masturbators whose health has
been injured immediately or consecutively, I can count *nine*
who were initiated into the practice at a place of public
education, and all I have read in other authors shows me that
this proportion is not exaggerated. The boy elevated in the
bosom of the family may be kept from circumstances which
will arouse his curiosity or awaken his desires ; such may
arise spontaneously or accidentally, but are not likely to produce a permanent effect except upon children of most ardent
temperament ; a thousand distractions arise to avert their
influence. At school these causes do not exist; but there are
others ; they are less numerous, less varied, but they act in a
more active manner and continue more permanently. Their
effects are direct and almst inevitable. The boy finds himself
in a very hotbed of contagion, which extends all around him
for the evil is established there in an epidemic form and is
transmitted without interruption, from the elder to the newer

comers. If some privileged few at first escape these per-
fidious initiations, it is those who come later. When the
senses begin to speak, the same objects will represent themselves to the memory under a less disgusting aspect.

CHAPTER VIII.

ANTIQUITY AND GENERAL PREVALENCE OF MASTURBATION,.

Another question, equally interesting, here presents itself.
What has been the influence of the progress of civilization on
abuses of the organs of generation ?

This question, very grave and highly complex has frequently
been lightly treated, and to get a clear idea of the matter, it
is necessary to examine, without prejudice, all its aspects, and
carefully distinguish between things which have always been
confounded. This is what I shall try to do because, at the
root of what may be considered as purely speculative, facts
may be found having an application of great practical
importance.

Masturbation seems, in ancient times, never to have produced the ravages which are marked by its extent now. It is
never alluded to in the Bible, for the conduct of Onan with
his brother's wife had not the least resemblance to this vice,
and yet we find in the pages of Holy Writ things more scandalous than masturbation, they are given in long detail and
in the plainest terms. It is not then from discretion that
the sacred writers have abstained from speaking of it. The

Greeks have left us nothing on this passion, those who have treated lightly and even with indulgence on an infamy very much more disgusting. Hippocrates has perfectly described the daily pollutions which took place among the newly married and the libertines, but neither here nor elsewhere do we find a word of masturbation.

Suetonius, Perseus, Juvenal have concealed nothing of Roman vice, but they have not named this. Galen and Celsus are also silent on the subject. It is scarcely a century since public attention, by isolated observations, has been called to its unhappy effects.

Masturbation appears then specially to have effected modern society, and its ravages seem ever on the increase.

With the Greeks and the Romans, the gymnasia played an immense role in education. The beauty of the human form was a special feature of culture, and sexual desires could with ease be naturally gratified. But masturbation is incompatible with physical force, with grace, with address, and was not likely to develop itself, except in default of other pleasures. It then had not commenced to slaughter its innumerable victims.

When Christianity came to purify the dissolute manners of the conquerors of the world, the chastity of its devotees was sustained by an ardent enthusiasm, by an inextinguishable faith, which made them brave torture and despise death. The most egotistic and degrading passion was not able to approach men who vowed to endure every persecution to propagate their belief.

Soon after numerous Barbarian invasions occurred, the days of chivalry and the rule of feudalism—that is to say war in all its forms, the reign of might and bravery. Each man's safety then depended upon the preservation of his strength and health. When something like order was established among all these troubles, the power rested in the hands of men armed in steel, whose warlike education commenced in infancy and was as rude as it was athletic.

As soon as the regime of violence and devastation was moderated revolutions of communities commenced; in this war of the oppressed against the oppressors force and energy were not less necessary than in the war between neighboring states.

At length, when the aristocracy, decimated by Richelieu and bastardized by Louis XIV., found in the court a great laxity of manners covered with a thin lacquer of gallantry. Louis XV. himself, and his regent with him, gave an example of debauchery the most flagrant; from the court it descended little by little and infected society in general. In this state of universal dissolution sexual exchange was too easy to leave many chances for the development of solitary vices.

All concurred then to prevent masturbation from making the ravages which it does in our day.

We must, therefore, regard this passion as a flower of modern growth. But must we, on this account, blame civilization? How could civilization produce such an effect? Was it in favoring the development of intelligence, the dissemination of knowledge? It is incontestable that masturbation leads to a diminution of intelligence, of memory, etc., and it is not less certain that the predominance of the noblest faculties of man is the surest guarantee that can be found against such shameful inclination. Everybody knows that among masturbators the most persistent and incorrigible are found in the least intelligent. Numerous examples of this might be adduced; idiots from birth, cretins, hydro-cephalees, who have just arrived at puberty. Let us descend to the nests of monkeys for reason and will; they are not able to master their bad habits. Everybody being agreed on this point I will not insist further.

It is favored by the increase of luxury and the accumulation of large numbers in cities. I know that this is the grand argument of those who charge to civilization the ravages of *chiromania*. Seduced by the paradoxical eloquence of Rosseau, these authors yet oppose, with the greatest confidence, the innocence of country manners to the corruption of the great cities. Not to reply to these vague declamations by denial without proof, I will select from the annals of medical art some facts bearing immediately on this question.

Chopart, in his treatise on maladies of the urinary organs, mentions many examples of stones in the bladder formed around some foreign substance. Setting aside those gathering about fragments of sounds and bougies which have been introduced merely to facilitate the flow of urine, we will take such cases about which there can be no manner of doubt as to the intention, and which have nearly all been observed among peasants. Take for example the young peasant who introduced into the urethra a large needle by the advice of a shepherd; another one who being seated under a grape vine took a slender tendril with which to pollute himself and provoke the ejaculation of semen; the laborer from whom Dr. Morgagin took a stone formed round a pin; the shepherd who had one developed round a piece of stick which he had introduced into the urethra to provoke pleasures that more horrible means were not able to produce as of yore.

On the other side, Morgagin reports a great number of examples of accidents noticed among the women from the in-

troduction of various strange articles. This is not the place
to examine these facts, but I wish to remark that almost all
these young women were of the peasant class.

I am able to add to these facts very many analagous observations, but it seems unnecessary. In all ages the poets, the
philosophers, the romancers, have taken pastoral life as the
type of their moral Utopias; this life has, to them, appeared
nearer to the Golden Age, but it is an illusion, for there has
never been such depravity as existed among shepherds and
shepherdesses.

When flocks are guarded by children of opposite sex, discoveries are rapidly made and intimate relations established,
long before the arrival of puberty. When many shepherds
are habitually together the disorders are not less. The
younger ones are contaminated by the elders, and laziness
gives to their passions a high degree of intensity and impu-
dence. A friend of mine one day, botanizing at Cevennes,
surprised in the middle of a wood six young shepherds seated
in a ring, giving themselves over to the manual pleasure in
the faces of each other. His opportune arrival scarcely made
them desist, and they showed more anger at being disturbed
than shame at having been surprised. The age of the eldest
of these miserable masturbators was but just that of puberty.

I will add to this the case of the young shepherdess treated
by Dr. Alibert. Living almost entirely isloated, she concealed
herself in the bushes and most retired places, and gave way
to an irresistible impulse. Her excesses were carried to the
verge of idiocy and to a nervous susceptibility, of which
nymphomania offers very few examples. She was discharged
after all coercive measures had been ineffectually tried. Never,
perhaps, with either sex, has brutality been pushed so far as

with these disgusting beings, *separated from the luxury and the corruption of great cities.* If the annals of science are consulted, we may easily assure ourselves that the most remarkable examples of shameful extravagances are furnished by individuals living in solitude and idleness.

If it should be objected that the corruptions of modern times are extended to the valleys and most solitary places, it will be easy to demonstrate that the manners of ancient shepherds were not more pure. Open Theocritus,. that eloquent model of rustic poetry, you will find details which I dare not even indicate. They must be sought for in the original, for translators have found it impossible to put them into a modern tongue. Let it suffice that women go for nothing in the passions of these shepherds—their jealousies, quarrels and reconciliations. Virgil is a little more guarded, though he does not hesitate to indicate similar turpitude. And what is remarkable about it, both of these writers speak of these things without disgust, without anger. They have written in praise of this country life, and not to amuse idlers after a debauch, so that the pictures they draw must be looked upon as a faithful description of the pastoral manners of the time.

In despoiling them of the rust of antiquity which has protected them, we see that these manners were worse than those of the shepherds of our day, since they practiced bestiality and sodomy, without scandal. This shows then that we cannot accuse modern civilization.

That which has led astray all the writers on masturbation is that they have only seen this vice without troubling themselves about others. But the real question is, are our manners more depraved than those of the ancients, than those of modern times where civilization has not so much advanced?

The historical facts which I shall pass in review will terminate the discussion.

I need not recall the history of Sodom and Gomorrah, nor the
astonishing details which are found in a hundred places in
the Bible. Although taking them without prejudice, we shall
be very little disposed to regret the ignorance of the patriarchs
and the morality of the elect. Similar vices have infected all
pagan antiquity with an immodesty which, in our day, it is
impossible to conceive. The gravest philosophers, the most
eminent men, those the most revered, have spoken of these
things without emotion. Some have even examined the
advantage of them in military discipline and social friendship
in the connection between tutor and pupil, etc. We well
know what important parts were played by the courtesans of
Athens, Corinth, etc. How sexual acts were favored by
public institutions, and even by religious communities. We
have read of the worship of Pallas, the mysteries of the
bonne déesse, etc., in the palmiest days of Greece and Rome.
Who would wish to see such disorders appear in the midst of
modern society ? What have we to envy in the manners of
the ancients ?

As to the nations we know best to-day, if it were possible
to pass them in review it could be easily demonstrated that
purity of manners is in direct ratio with the civilization, light
and liberty which they enjoy. If refuge is taken in a state
of nature, I would refer to a library of travels. It will be
seen how very little importance is attached by savages to the
sexual act. The women are in a complete state of abject
slavery, and the only value of virtue in them is the making
a traffic of it. It may be bought for an iron ring, a string of
beads or a bit of a mirror. I would ask them if we should go

back to those primitive manners even if we were able, who
would desire it ?

The result of all these facts observed on immense numbers,
in all times, in all countries, is that the adult man is drawn
towards the opposite sex by imperious desires, continuous and
inevitable, and by a blind instinct, which overrules all his
reasoning faculties ; that his conformation permits him easily
to abuse the organs of generation, when it is impossible for
him to legitimately use them ; that when his impulses are
checked in one direction, they will break out in another.

CHAPTER IX.

FURTHER EVILS OF SELF-ABUSE.

Christianity has extirpated the most infamous vice of antiquity ; for which thanks are due. In arousing a more
severe moral condition it has awakened noble sentiments in
both sexes ; it has purified the passions. Society owes all to
it. But it is not sufficient to preach anathemas against the
flesh to get rid of the prick in the flesh.

Some contagious maladies have appeared to check the most
gross sensual debauches ; but in admitting that these dangers
may, to some extent, restrain the greatest libertinage, these
fears change nothing ; they cannot change the organization
of mankind ; if these impulses override almost insurmountable obstacles, it is still not able to cause a revolt of the
senses. If it is repulsed on all sides, it is compelled to fall
back upon its own resources.

It is necessary to consider these facts fairly and compar-
atively to get an idea of all the evils caused by the abuse of
the genital organs.

Doubtlessly we may derive powerful help from assiduous
watching, from culture and intelligence, as well as from moral
and religious principles, but all these means are weak against
practices so easily concealed, and which are always at the
disposition of such as care to use them. Something more is
necessary; it is desirable, as much as possible, to stifle the
desire by occupations as varied as possible, and which will
thoroughly weary the body.

The effects of regular, habitual, energetic exercise are so
great and so unknown that I wish to insist upon the necessity
of introducing into all colleges and schools gymnastic exercises, of which so little has been known since the invention
of firearms.

I will now enter on some details of certain acts which exercise a most dangerous influence on the genital organs, putting
aside all which has not some practical application of importance.

I have already alluded to the danger of compressing the
urethra during ejaculation to prevent the expulsion of the
semen. One of my patients writes me : " From fourteen
years of age I gave myself up to masturbation, three or four
times a week, and sometimes as frequent as that in one day.
To prevent the emission I squeezed tightly the root of the
penis. I saw nothing escaped at the moment, which reassured
me, but later I noticed semen coming out with the urine the
first time I emitted such after the act. These precautions
I took for about two years. Daily pollutions were not slow in
making their appearance and provoking symptoms more and

more grave. The rest of this observation contains nothing which has not been noticed in other cases, but what I wished to remark was, that the compression was exercised at the mouth of the ejaculatory canals, and that the patient believed for a long time that his manœuvres were not followed by seminal loss, until he was cruelly undeceived.

Fournier and Begin report a similar case of a young man who at the moment of ejaculation compressed the most retreating part of the urethra in such a manner as to prevent the escape of one drop of semen. Notwithstanding the consequences were the same as in ordinary cases. In spite of precautions, the forces diminished and weakness ensued just as rapidly as if the seminal evacuation had been completed.

Of another very remarkable case I will allow the patient to give the details:

"I am thirty-two years old, and have had nocturnal pollutions, from my fourteenth year. As to losses when at stool, such date back some ten years. The cause of these pollutions was not masturbation, since I have not indulged in such twenty times in my life. They are rather due to the reading of lascivious books, for they commenced immediately after.

In the beginning the ejaculation was preceded by dreams, accompanied by very powerful erections, sensations more or less lively, and the seed was ejected with force; I cannot tell you all the plans I have tried to get rid of them. I have, during the whole night kept my penis soaking in cold water or compressed between two pieces of wood made for the purpose. I tried not to sleep because no emissions took place in a wakeful state, and the next day I would feel stronger, but at the end of some days drowsiness would overpower me. I occasionally succeeded in awakening myself before coming to the

catastrophe, but was generally too late ; then to restrain the
loss or to render it less abundant, I compressed the base of the
penis powerfully, but it appeared that these compressions
have fatigued the parts without diminishing the flow, which
had taken place behind as I came to find out when I had examined my urine. Since that epoch the pollutions have not
been preceded by dreams, the sensations have disappeared so
that it has been impossible to arouse myself, the erections
have diminished or ceased entirely. For three years it has
been rarely that they have accompanied the pollutions ; when
they do I am less fatigued.

One thing will, I doubt not, appear absurd to you as a
physical impossibility, which is that I have experienced the
pollutions without erections, without sensation and without
the semen being expelled from the mouth of the urethra. I
have always thought that it was carried into the bladder by a
retrograde movement, and there became mingled with the
urine ; since the next day I have found many little globules,
a cloudiness and some filaments, as when I hindered the emission by the compression of the base of the penis, while there
would be nothing of the kind in the urine during the day or
in the morning when I had during the night no pollutions. I
always knew when they had taken place by the perspiration
in which I awoke, by the lassitude, the black circles round my
eyes, and the pain in the head, although my linen would be
without a stain.

Every time when I have been able to pass a night without
sleeping, my urine would be transparent in the morning and I
would feel strong. After many nights without sleep I have
ordinarily an energetic pollution which fatigues me but little,
but whenever they came on without erection, without exterior
evacuation, I have felt tired and weary in the morning."

I fancy many medical men have not been able to realize these pollutions without exterior evacuation, since they scarcely admit that the seed can escape without pleasure, but the patient really experienced interior pollutions without any apparent evacuation ; that is to say the semen was forced backward into the bladder and escaped with the urine, as where previously it had been arrested by the pinching of the perineum.

This compression was exercised in front of the ejaculatory vessels ; it was frequently repeated. It is then very probable that the frequency of these maneuvers has finished by leading to a spontaneous deviation of sperm into the bladder, so much more so as the patient has at the time perceived that they fatigued the canal. To this question I shall recur.

However this may be, all the maneuvers do not much differ from the mechanical means recommended by some physicians to prevent nocturnal pollutions. It will be seen how little confidence is to be placed in these instruments and the inconveniences they present.

A singular error seems to have crept into Dr. Deslande's work when he says : That the application of splints, laces, etc., to the penis is done with lubricous intent. It is not erotic delirium which leads to these imprudences, but a lively desire to suppress nocturnal emissions. This explanation my patients give to me, and I find it plausible, for accidents are not produced except by the swelling of the penis, which proves that it was not in a state of erection when these applications have been made. The reflections of Dr. Deslande's have probably been suggested by the fact which he states before, and which I reproduce : A young man presented himself at the clinic of the Hotel Dieu, carrying the ferule

of a candlestick on his penis, before which the glans penis
had enormously swelled. No efforts would seem to remove
this strange circlet. Strong pincers and a filing away of the
cylinder were necessary to remove it. All these circumstances
are very exact, but I must add that having been charged to
interrogate the patient, I found that he was reduced by nocturnal pollutions, and it was in the hope to prevent them
that he had put the piece of candlestick round his penis. I
believed his statement from the simple fact that his member
could never have been got through the iron tube if it had not
been in a state of the most complete flaccidity.

I will add a few other aberrations which have been avowed
to me by other patients. One of them told me that at the
advent of puberty, suspending himself one day by the arms,
he had experienced a prompt and energetic erection, accompanied by pleasure, and that in his endeavors to raise his
body he had emitted an abundant jet of semen. It was his
first emission. The next day he repeated the same movements, and observed exactly the same phenomenon. From
that time he knew no other pleasure. From the principles
which had been instilled in his youth he would have believed
himself dishonored by having any connection with a woman,
or if he had permitted the slightest liberties with his person;
but his conscience was tranquil relative to these exercises,
because he had never heard them forbidden. He therefore
continued to suspend himself to pieces of furniture, doors, or
anything which came handy, without taking any one into
confidence, and fell little by little into that state of weakness
and despondency which marks the worst class of masturbators. At last all suspension became impossible from feebleness, and the voluntary emissions ceased, but were immedi-

ately replaced by nocturnal pollutions which were difficult to
cure, as the organs of generation had become disposed to them
by this peculiar practice.

Another patient detailed as follows : " Endowed with a very
precocious temperament, I abused myself from the age of
eight or nine years, if not exactly by masturbation, yet by
maneuvers still more hurtful. It was by the compression of
my penis against my thigh, or against the chair on which I
was sitting, that I provoked the pleasurable sensations, ordinarily followed by the escape of some drops of a sticky and
transparent liquid. This practice, which I repeated many
times a day, lasted until I was about sixteen, when I ceased
entirely, alarmed by the emission of blood which I noticed
followed the operation, almost pure. Since that period I have
only sought natural pleasures, but I have been unable to obtain
them, as in the presence of a woman I could not secure a perfect erection ; this state, attributed to feebleness, has only
been up to this time combated by tonics, by excitants, and
by irritations of every description, which, in their turn, have
worked much evil."

I knew a military officer who had fallen into the same state
by following similar practices; except that it was against the
leg of a table that he secured his earliest sensations, at the
age of ten, while engaged at his devotions, and he continued
for many years to employ the same means.

I have seen other invalids with whom riding on horseback
had provoked the first seminal loss.

I have already spoken of the danger arising from permitting infants to go to sleep upon their bellies, but I may add
that many of my patients have in this manner contracted
habits which have ruined their health. Independently of

the inconvenience of this method of reclining for restoration and digestion, it favors erections, and the onward march is rapid when once the way is discovered. One of my consultants said that he would rather die than have sullied his nature by a single amorous touch on the parts of generation; and, notwithstanding, for five or six years he had rarely passed a night without securing the same result by lying upon his belly.

I will not perpetuate the evils by speaking of other and more lascivious methods by which many have conciliated their genital instincts with the moral and religious principles which had been inculcated during childhood, simply remarking that if they have succeeded in deceiving their consciences they have not preserved their health; and which still more confirms what I have said of the insufficiency of these principles when they are not seconded by bodily fatigue.

CHAPTER X.

INDIRECT SELF-ABUSE AND ITS CONSEQUENCES.

It is not, at all times, sufficient to abstain from direct action on the sexual organs to preserve them from grave disorders. A purely nervous excitement, awakened by the other senses or directly provoked by lascivious thoughts, will produce the same effects as the more brutal manipulations, if they lead to too prolonged erections, too frequently repeated, of which I will give a few examples:

A Swiss student, twenty-two years of age, of sanguine temperament and Herculean build, fell into a state of the most complete impotency from having passed for more than a year, sometime almost every night, tete-a-tete with his affianced; he had constantly respected her and was not addicted to any solitary practice, but the violent and prolonged erections which resulted from the perfect intimacy renewed themselves during the day under the influence of the memory, and these fatiguing erections led to frequent and abundant nocturnal pollutions. Absence removed the dangerous contact but not the consequences. The pollution diminished little by little, even ceasing entirely, but not before the young man had fallen into the same state of impotence as the most inveterate masturbator, although preserving an appearance of health and strength. It was easy for me upon examining his urine to discover the cause of the loss of virility, and engaging him to carefully note what occurred at stool, but the cure of these diurnal pollutions occupied two years.

I have met with a similar case in a young man who passed successively from a state of habitual priapism to the most absolute impotence, from no other cause than the constant excitement of the genital organs from violent passion, although he had never given way to secret excesses of any kind. I also attended a young English officer who left Calcutta full of vigor and arrived in London completely impotent, after having experienced during two months almost constant erections; they were provoked by a young widow, very coquette, but colder still, who amused herself by arousing but never allaying his passions. His weakness lasted more than two years, uninterrupted by a sign of virility. It is almost needless to add that he suffered from involuntary seminal emissions. I have else-

where alluded to nocturnal pollutions evoked by the reading
of lascivious books. I have under my eye many observations
of this kind, but they are not accompanied by circumstances
of sufficient importance to merit special mention. I conclude
from these, that with certain very impressionable individuals
the reading of erotic works, the sight of voluptuous pictures,
lascivious conversations, in a word, all the sensations liable to
provoke excitement of the spermatic organs, are able to produce the same effects as abuse or manual excesses, that even
when the will is sufficiently powerful it will lead these
thoughts to the completing of the sexual act; at any rate
there is sure to result a more abundant secretion of semen,
more importunate erections, irritations of the urethra and of
the prostrate, etc., which favor the development of nocturnal
pollutions; then daily, quite as grave and more difficult to
arrest, because it is more difficult to act medicinally on the
memory and the imagination. It will not do then to charge
all material action on the genital organs; it is necessary to
avoid all erotic excitement in the senses, all concentration of
thought on lascivious subjects. Unhappily Fortune's favors
have been so irregularly divided that they permit a crowd of
useless beings to exist in a state of perfect idleness without
incurring anybody's blame as they ask nothing from anybody.
The only remedy I know for this inaction is that we look
upon and treat the laziness of the rich with as much disgust
as we do the begging habits of the poor; it is only the daily
fatigue of body which will aid it to escape varied excesses.

The effects produced by different abuse vary according to
the age, the individual and the organs of the sexual economy.
Examined under these divers points of view they are able to
furnish matter for serious and important consideration, but

I must here neglect all which is commonly known and all which elsewhere I shall be called upon to describe.

I have insisted in a special manner on the causes which are able to provoke bad habits long before the arrival of puberty, I must now treat of their effects during that period of life. The symptoms produced by masturbation on the adult and the infant have always been confounded, notwithstanding they present some distinct traits, which give to them peculiar aspects, and we are made aware of these differences by some consequences which it is necessary to examine.

However young children may be they become thin, pale and difficult to manage, their sleep is short, agitated and interrupted, and if the evil habit is not arrested, will finally succumb. So many terminations of youthful existence from these causes are recorded that I need not particularize. Analogous symptoms are manifested in the adult moving in the same line and coming to the same termination. But in infancy there are nervous accidents more or less grave which we do not find with those who make their debut after the period of puberty, where are not noticed, at least in the same degree, spasmodic contractions, partial convulsions, epilepsy and a species of paralysis, accompanied by the contraction of the members. These spasmodic phenomena are remarked in all infants addicted to the vice so far as my researches go. As soon as we are able to entirely master the passion with infants it becomes easy to establish health, and it may be done rapidly. I have always noticed with what facility the gravest symptoms have disappeared. Dr. Deslandes has been struck by the rapidity of the changes and remarks on the power of nature's resources and these observations must modify the common opinion that infancy is life's epoch where these abuses are the most dangerous, on account of the nutrition of the body and the susceptibility of the nervous system. If the effects are rapid and serious, they cease as promptly when the cause is removed, and the re-establishment is certain.

What is said of infants is also true of women. It is easy to be convinced of this in noticing the observations on the excision of the clitoris with nymphomaniacs. The state of those unhappy women to whom such an extreme measure was absolutely necessary must have been deplorable, and, notwithstanding, all seem to have been very promptly cured.

Why, in these cases, is the cure so certain and re-established health so rapid when once the unhappy passion is mastered? It is that all the causes of enfeeblement cease as soon as the habit is conquered. Why do so many men continue to fail in strength after they have completely corrected the evil practice? Because to them is left diurnal pollution, more debilitating still than the practices of which it is the result.

I must here notice an error into which all writers on masturbation seem to have fallen. They report examples of adults arrived at the last degree of seminal impotence whose health is re-established very rapidly as soon as the destructive habit is conquered, while others continue to lead the most deplorable life, although the habit has been corrected for a long period, and in a manner absolute, for I speak now of men separated from female intercourse ; I will even add that they do not discover any nocturnal pollutions. These facts, in appearance contradictory, cause some medical writers to say that masturbators are soon renovated when the vice is conquered, and others, that this renovation is sometimes difficult and even impossible, and they attribute this lack of improvement to the profound alteration of the economy of the nervous system, etc., although many of the patients reported cured have been in a worse state.

That which is not less remarkable than the rapid decline, says Dr. Deslandes, is the facility with which flesh is gained by the greater number of masturbators when they have been induced to suspend their maneuvers. While some individuals remain all their lives weak, dry and withered from the abuse to which they have, during their youth, abandoned themselves. Although the doctor has remarked the difference, he has not sought for its explanation.

If it should be asked why some remain victims to daily pollutions while others are exempt, it must be stated that one has been duped by an illusion, confounding cases which do not at all resemble each other. The fact is, one class have triumphed over their bad habits by the force of their will, the other have renounced it from impotence. The first have resisted their desire while yet powerful, possessing sufficient courage to triumph over it; the others have merely relaxed their efforts to procure pleasure when the solicitation has become less, and the progressive depreciation of their erections has been due to daily and unperceived pollutions.

In some the genital organs are sound, the constitution intact—there are no seminal losses, except those which are voluntarily produced; the soundness of the digestive organs permit prompt reparation. But as soon as the constant irritation has weakened, chronically, the spermatic organs, an abundant quantity of semen escapes day by day, many times a day in fact, without the victim realizing the loss, digestion becomes deranged, erections diminish as well as voluptuous sensations, because the seed is less elaborated; dangerous provocations cease little by little, and the invalid easily renounces habits which no longer inspire any feeling but disgust. Then he thinks himself virtuous, and is astonished that his health continues to decline, because he is not aware that he is losing more semen in a day by imperceptible evacuations, but frequently repeated, than he expended at any time by his manual operations. We must not then confound those whose virility has abandoned them with those who have triumphed by the power of the will, or be surprised to see the change of conduct in both, following different and even opposite phenomena.

I could quote many illustrative cases, but will merely specify some of the obstacles which oppose the execution of the best intentions conceived by very many masturbators.

After some days of absolute forbearance, purchased with a mass of precautions, they frequently experience nocturnal pollutions, the more frequent and the more abundant as the organs have been the more irritated, and they are generally more affected by these involuntary losses than by those which they had hitherto procured for themselves. In place of combating them by legitimate means, or after having tried some such without immediate success, they believe they are able to diminish the evil in seeking to replace these involuntary losses by others less frequent, and thus take up again with their former habits, thus further augmenting the irritation of the spermatic organs. Then come the diurnal pollutions which ruin them, but as they do not perceive them they felicitate themselves on the progressive disappearance of their nightly emissions. Notwithstanding, their health gets worse daily; then they understand nothing more, and finish by believing that they have deceived themselves as to the true cause of their maladies.

Connection with women has generally been advised in sim-

ilar cases, and with a show of reason, for examples of its
success are not wanting, but it is with this means as with all
others.   It is first necessary to show that it can be used, and
if so to distinguish the circumstances in which it may be
advantageous or otherwise.

Very many sufferers have attempted this remedy, merely to
find their utter incompetence to carry it to a satisfactory termination.   They, perhaps, take a disgust at the only females
within their reach for such a purpose, or fear compromising
their health, and the females are in the same condition ; with
other women they have a feeling of respect or scruples of
conscience ; the women fear a pregnancy or a scandal ; the
immodesty of one class revolts them, the reserve of another
repulses them ; there only remains marriage, and they see too
well, in their semi-impotent state, the unhappy result of such
a union.   The numerous confidences of this sort I have received appear full of truth.   Sometimes in entering into the
most secret details I have discovered that trials had shown
impotency more or less declared, and that such incompetency
was the result of daily pollutions, of which fact the invalids
had later recognized the importance.

Many writers have remarked the indifference, in some cases
amounting to aversion, of masturbators for women.   This
sentiment is in truth very common with those who have gone
to extreme lengths in self-abuse; but I do not think it can be
referred to the protracted habit of solitary pleasure; at least
I am able to assign to this aversion a cause more direct.   I wish
to speak of the relative impotency into which these invalids
fall.   I call it relative, because while they can secure a sufficient erection to manipulate themselves, they are not able to
get up a stiffness which would secure them from certain

shame, and what proves that this is the fear which governs
them is that they only show these sentiments with regard to
women after having failed, and the remembrance follows
them; it is also seen that they completely change the manner
of looking at coition with a woman when the diurnal pollutions have been checked which led to this impotence and on
which these fears were founded. The effects of genital abuse
vary very much in their intensity and character according to
the individuals. Some will resist for a long time the most
frightful masturbation, while others will be rapidly affected.
I have, in this regard, seen the greatest contrasts and all the
intermediate shades. Temperament seems to have very little
to do with this irregularity of resistance. The strength or
weakness of the constitution does not seem to affect it so
much as might be imagined. The very unequal vigor of the
genital organs seems alone to give a satisfactory explanation.
As I shall have similar observations to make when I come to
speak of venereal excesses, I shall omit them here to avoid
repetition.

In the same individual all the organs are not equally affected
by the same abuse, as proved by the frequent predominance
of certain symptoms which give to the physiognomy peculiar
characteristics, which lead to grave errors in diagnosis.
Blennorrhœa is more common than usually supposed with
masturbators. Retention of the urine more or less prolonged
is a frequent feature. Inflammation of the bladder is a
common result of masturbation, with patients who have
pushed their madness to an extreme point. Bloody emissions
are common, even to the urinating of almost pure blood.
Incontinence of urine is common with young masturbators.
Acute inflammation of the testicles has followed masturbating

maneuvers pushed to an extreme, and continued frequently, with a kind of erotic madness. The testicles secrete a greater quantity of semen, but it is not so thoroughly elaborated. The seminal vessels have more difficulty in retaining it. They contract more easily as they become more impressionable, and from this cause nocturnal pollutions become harder and harder to cure, and daily pollutions more frequent and abundant, that is to say, there is a disposition always increasing for contraction on the part of the seminal vessels for the expulsion of the sperm.

On the other side, already badly elaborated by the testicles, remaining briefly in its reservoirs it becomes more and more aqueous; in a measure it loses its physiological character, and also its normal properties; it becomes less apt to produce its effects on the seminal vessels, the erections become less energetic, less durable, more incomplete, capricious and fugitive, and finally, in desperate cases, disappear altogether.

From thence the embarrassment, the timidity of these unhappy people in the presence of women, the fear of placing themselves in a position where their impotence must at once be discovered; from thence, also, their indifference, even their aversion for the sex, and the difficulty always present which opposes itself to a change of habit.

Abuse, it is thus seen, provokes symptoms of which the cause cannot be ascertained, because they persist after the evil itself has been long corrected. Some continue to waste away, while others are re-established as soon as they renounce their passion. These symptoms explain why tonics, aphrodisiacs, cold baths and acid drinks, produce at times far different effects from what are intended.

There are, doubtless, cases in which the sexual organs are

enfeebled, relaxed, but it will be seen that these follow a
primitive disposition, above all in the default of normal exercise for these organs, rather than an abuse of them. When
such alone produce diurnal pollutions, it is in developing in
the organs a state of vital energy more or less pronounced,
more or less stubborn.

The facts I shall review also permit an explanation of the
contradictions we meet with in authors relating to the influence of masturbation on the sensitiveness of the organs of
generation. Many pretend that this sensitiveness is very
much augmented with masturbators, while others affirm that
it is diminished, and being thus divided in their opinions they
are continually contradicting each other and themselves.

This incoherence comes from the confounding of things
perfectly distinct, and even opposite ; these judge the sensibility of the genital parts by the domination of voluptuous
sensations, those by the acceleration of the ejaculations, by
the susceptibility the parts acquire, and the pains to which
they are subject. But the differences observed in the same
individual in the liveliness of the pleasure is essentially owing to the degree of elaboration which the semen has under-
gone in the seminal vessels ; but masturbation and the pollutions which take place in consequence of it, are opposed to a
prolonged stay of the semen ; in effect, the more irritation
increases the pathological sensitiveness the more promptly
is the sperm expelled, the waterier it becomes, and the sensitiveness, or rather the sensation, is enfeebled.

It is rightly said that masturbation was the most dangerous
vice, because it is more difficult to discover, to determine, to
combat, on account of its being a solitary vice, etc. I must
add that the irritation provoked by these brutal maneuvers

leads more easily to involuntary seminal losses ; that the appearance of nocturnal pollutions, with those who attempt to restrain from the long-practiced vice, frequently leads to a return to the old habits ; that the diminution of vitality, far from favoring the amendment of the unhappy sufferer, is sometimes acting in a contrary direction, in putting obstacles to the commerce with woman without tending to deliver them from their bondage to the destroying habit.

The fatal slavery of these last circumstances is the most irresistible of evils which attend those who permit themselves to be prisoners in this charmed but vicious circle.

I regard as excess all venereal acts pushed beyond the real requirements. This explanation may appear useless at the moment, but it will be seen that it is more difficult and more important than may be thought to know exactly what constitutes an excess, and by what signs we are to recognize it as such.

Dr. Deslandes signifies by venereal act all exercise of the organs of generation accompanied by pleasure. This extension of the etymological sense continually leads to confusion. It is to be desired that we had some general word to indicate all normal or abnormal employment of these organs, but it would be better to create one than to call masturbation, sodomy, bestiality, etc., venereal acts, for there is certainly nothing appertaining to Venus in exercises in which no woman takes a part.

EFFECTS OF ONANISM, OR WITHDRAWAL.

CHAPTER XI.

ON OTHER SEXUAL EXCESSES.

I will now proceed to relate a few examples of venereal excess. M. B. was small, thin, nervous in character, and of a warm and firm temperament. He had escaped all bad habits and had never had any connection with women. At the age of twenty-one he married a charming young lady with whom he was desperately in love, and during eighteen months he used his conjugal rights four or five times a day. At length coition became so habitual in him that he gave way to it during sleep, only awakening at the denoucment.

At the commencement all his functions had taken on a great activity—he was gay, hearty, and his appetite, above all, was augmented in a remarkable manner. But this condition diminished little by little, giving way to a contrary condition; his sleep was short and non-refreshing, he was drowsy in the daytime, his appetite failed, his flesh diminished as did his intellectual activity and his muscular power. His temper became restless, impatient, irascible.

Pregnancy ensuing, these symptoms disappeared, but reappeared some months after his wife's confinement and augmented in a rapid way. The use of succulent and abundant food in place of repairing his powers produced indigestion; exciting drinks taken as stomachics merely irritated. An obstinate constipation followed, and was succeeded by a still more dispiriting diarrhea. At the same time his venereal desires became equally enfeebled. Erections diminished, ejaculation was more easily induced, and provoked but little sensation. Coition was now many days and sometimes for one or two weeks omitted.

A second pregnancy led to some months of absolute repose, but this time renewed health did not follow. Nocturnal pollutions, which he regarded as the consequence of enforced continence, set in, but coition, though rare, failed to cure but rather augmented the weakness; the nocturnal pollutions then diminished, disappeared completely, while the palpitations were increased as were also the digestive derangements.

It was now that he remarked during the expulsion of fecal matter a thick, viscous, unctuous, slightly opaque matter escape from the urethra, frequent emission of urine, a very little each time and with very small force, the last drop thick and sticky, with pains in the spermatic cords and testicles, and spasmodic contractions between the sphincter of the anus and the neck of the bladder. This was his condition when he came to me, but it was a long time, even with the application of my Nervine and other remedies, before his condition was ameliorated. When he ceased to be a patient the diurnal pollutions had ceased, some nocturnal pollutions took place but accompanied by dreams, the erections being strong and the pleasure great; erotic desires were again awakened, and his need of coition imperious. He was soon as well as ever; for ten years he has had the full exercise of his powers, and past experience has made him circumspect.

In this case there was not the least complication. The first sexual experiences commenced all at once at the age of twenty-one years, the constitution was robust, the genital organs had been preserved from all abuse, the orgasms which were excited were in the highest degree, and the whole being received a lively excitation at this novel era of pleasure and happiness; during some time all the functions were executed with the greatest energy, losses were promptly repaired, and health was retained in all its vigor. Where, then, was danger to be suspected ? Would not the past answer for the future ? Was it easy to arrest the passions when every sense spoke so energetically, when the seductions were inevitable, when pride and self-esteem were in the balance ? Habit alone could restrain this excess, since the influences at work mastered the will.

The wife's pregnancy allowed the first attacks to disappear because they were merely the result of venereal excesses. A second pregnancy failed so to do because diurnal pollutions had already been developed.

Conjugal excesses are worthy of special note under all circumstances, for they attack the very foundations of society ; and those who are most exposed to them are the youngest husbands, the least experienced the most passionate ; those whose previous character has been the most regular ; and yet these cases are so common that it is needless to multiply examples.

All excess is an immoderate, and therefore harmful use of a thing useful within reasonable limits. It is under these two aspects that the act of generation must be examined to secure a complete idea ; it is this also which essentially distinguishes it from all genital abuses, which never can produce advantageous results, however rarely they may be practiced.

But how is it to be determined when the natural sexual act is to be regarded as moderate, as useful, or at least as without danger ? Where does excess commence, that is to say, injurious frequency ? These important questions have never been resolved in a satisfactory manner. They have, in fact, never been proposed.

In this evolution, each one consulting his own experience, has arrived at different conclusions. The power of activity in the sexual organs differs widely in individuals; they vary at different times with the same individuals. No other organ of the animal economy presents such an inequality. It thus becomes evident that all evolution given in fixed numbers must be illusory. It is only by the demand of the genital feeling that conclusions can be arrived at, but it is not easy to appreciate these demands which vary, following the age of individuals and a crowd of circumstances of which the combinations are infinite.

The genital demands may be exorbitant; a violent passion is able to cause, in this respect, great illusions. Direct irritation caused by preputial disease, by the presence of ascarides in the rectum, etc., may provoke morbid erections which are not real demands; an irritation of the cerebellum of the spinal marrow, or of the genital nerves may produce the same effects, so that the frequency and duration of a hardened penis are not always a faithful measure of real sexual demands.

With very many ardent men the genital instinct predominates over the sexual organs. Their imagination is occupied by lascivious ideas; their greediness is immense, but their physical means are feeble. The impulse with them is in the mind; their immoderate desires will not furnish the exact measure of the real demand. It is because they deceive themselves, that they lose themselves.

On the other hand, too absolute a continence, and too prolonged finishes by throwing the genital feeling into a state of inertia, of defect of muscular power, which might be taken for impotence, and which may lead to that condition.

Spermatic plethora, carried to the extreme, is usually accompanied by a sentiment of anxiety and general indisposition, headache, torpor, somnolence ; or of agitation, sleeplessness and impatience ; the character changes, becomes taciturn and melancholy, aptitude for work diminishes, then ensues physical and moral feebleness, disgust of life, love of solitude ; the spermatic cords are swollen, painful, as are also the testicles. These phenomena are noted in all young men arrived at puberty who have escaped bad habits and have had no sexual intercourse. They are not rare till forty or more years with those who have submitted to a deprivation of all sexual acts or other means of getting rid of the elaborated semen. Exaggerated and prolonged seminal losses are frequently accompanied by similar symptoms.

It may appear strange that such opposite causes should produce such similar effects, but facts show that any condition opposed to the true economy of nature produces corresponding phenomena.

However this may be, it is difficult to judge of the real wants of each individual *à priori*, since the frequency of the erections and their duration, the heat of venereal desires, and the phenomena observed in the different functions of the animal economy, all tend to lead to erroneous conclusions. It is still the same if we attempt to appreciate genital wants after the immediate effects of a venereal act. Then it is always easy to foresee the ulterior consequences which must wait for new sexual action.

There are signs which it is impossible to misunderstand, and which are applicable in all cases.

When connection with a woman is followed by a sentiment of joy, of general well being, of new vigor, when the head is lighter, the body more supple, when there is more disposition to exercise of body, to mental activity, and the genital organs, above all, manifest a renewal of vigor and activity, it is certain an imperious want has been satisfied within the necessary limits of health. The happy influence which all the organs share is similar to that which succeeds the accomplishment of any other function of the animal economy.

On the other hand, when coition is followed by a sense of weariness, of satiety, a throbbing in the head, a disposition to somnolence, a slowness in ideas, a sluggishness of action, an uncertainty of will, it may be certain that the act has been too much repeated, or at least effected under unfavorable circumstances, and it is merely a deception if after such coition more or less energetic erections should occur, for they are provoked by the commencement of irritation, not by a return of the natural want.

It is only when the act is followed by all these phenomena that it can be truthfully said : *post coitum animal triste* (after the act the animal is sad); it is then alone that it is injurious. In effect, sadness, regret, bad humor, only follow when the act has been too often repeated, or too lasciviously indulged in. This moral state suffices to indicate that there has been an excess, or an inopportunity, which will produce the same results.

These two orders of phenomena are rarely as striking as may be supposed, because the want is rarely sufficiently pressing, or the excess sufficiently grave, but there are few men of forty who have not experienced one or both. Intermediate cases between these two extremes constitute the ordinary train of life ; then sexual intercourse is not followed by any remarkable phenomena, from whence it may be concluded that in the immense majority of cases it is far from having the evil effects which are attributed to it.

I have thought it my duty to establish these facts thus precisely, because those who have written on the subject have put more or less exaggeration in their exposition of the effects of coition, being anxious to vividly affect the imaginations of their readers. They have also the same tendency to present the sexual act as constantly hurtful, admitting no difference from what follows the connection.

I do not speak here of the pure theoretical declamations which writers make, who pretend that *the creation of a new being* must necessarily operate at the expense of the party accomplishing the fact ; that each one of these acts destined to give new life must be an approach to death, etc. There is in all this pomp of style nothing beyond college eloquence and phrases for effect, which merit no serious attention. I shall merely speak of conscientious observers who have treated the subject scientifically.

CHAPTER XII.

NERVOUS EXCITEMENT AND STIMULATING CAUSES.

There are some who have applied themselves to the nervous question, that expenditure which must result from epileptiform contractions, by which the entire economy is agitated during the venereal act, on the importance of the semen, etc.;

they have cited, for example, the history of insects, where the males perish immediately after fecundation, without naming the bull, the cock, the goat, the stallion, where the organization approaches more nearly that of man; they have compiled medical works, and above all periodical collections to exhibit the most frightful examples of the pernicious effects of copulation; sudden death, apoplexy, epilepsy, blindness, etc., all have been put under contribution.

That the internal operations are interrupted during connection from the augmentation of the heart's action is not doubtful, and nothing is more easy to explain; but does not such occur from any other excitement? Does it not occur spontaneously?

It is true that apoplexy sometimes intervenes during the copulative act, and I could quote many examples, but would not any other violent exercise have produced the same results? How must we account for orators, lawyers, preachers, who have been struck down on the platform, in the court room, in the pulpit? How of plethoric individuals whom we have seen seized during a fit of anger, in an animated discussion, or even under the influence of a lively emotion? How of constipated individuals during the act of defecation? How of bon vivants during the digestion of a too luxurious meal?

Yet the greater part have been found in their bed without any other cause being assigned than the horizontal position; until then have they not every night slept with impunity in the same position? This determinate cause usually occurs at ages varying from fifty to sixty years. If we wish to apply the same reasoning to cases so common, the horizontal position must be regarded as a cause as common as copulation for bringing on apoplexy.

Venereal excesses, like all other debilitating causes, certainly dispose to nervous affections. When these convulsions immediately succeed the act of coition, it is evident that a predisposition to such accidents existed, and that any other excitement would have caused it. Epilepsy declares itself the first night of marriage, or the day after, can it be reasonably assigned to an excess in handselling the bride? In many of these cases the act has not even been consummated. These facts then cannot be used to prove the danger of copulation!

If it be thought useful to offer these things as a warning to the imprudent, who are tempted to abuse their sexual strength, I think it an erroneous opinion. I should fancy that such statements would be more likely to produce on the imagination of all readers a directly contrary impression. Those who are the most ignorant of medicine will make up their minds that theirs is an entirely different case—that similar effects must be attributed to an imminent predisposition which merely waited for an opportunity to make itself active. One excess risked, and all others become easy. Tissot's work would certainly have had more effect on educated men if he had omitted those extraordinary cases which are found there without selection and without criticism.

Unhappily they have not been abandoned by later writers, but on the contrary, analogous facts have been added ; if they were preserved they should certainly have been commented upon, and not left for general acceptance.

In addition to masturbation and other excesses, there are other causes which serve to produce involuntary seminal loss, whether carried to an extreme or hurtful in themselves. This subject I shall now examine.

The novel sensations which arise from the sensibility which

comes to the organs of generation at the epoch of puberty, the kind of habitual orgasm of which they become the seat, the confidence which is given by an unaccustomed vigor, the want of experience, all lead the youth to allow his first desires to run riot. Sometimes, in our social system, this tendency finds obstacles sufficiently strong, sufficiently numerous to overcome them totally or partially. Complete successes were desirable, if the genital instinct under the compression were not liable to explode. However this may be, it is seldom that the ripe youth meets with circumstances favorable to habitual excess sufficient to destroy health. At least I have found very few cases compared with those arising from masturbation.

When the development of manhood is complete he finds more liberty; he is delivered from constraint, and gives full sway to his desires. But if venereal acts are more multiplied than at any other epoch, the virile power is also in all its energy, resistance to causes of deterioration is stronger; if the provocations do not come from the genital organs there would be no more true excess than at any other age, since the frequency of the copulations will be proportioned to the real wants. Later on genital power diminishes little by little, and finishes by extinction in old age; but the desires follow the same decreasing progression.

Thus the energy of the genitals at the epoch of the greatest virility will not provoke to actual excess if not stimulated by other causes; on the other hand their weakness will not render copulation more dangerous but more rare.

The preponderance of the lymphatic temperament renders the animal economy less proper to bear venereal excess, but then this temperament is less disposed to indulge than the others. All other things being equal, the lymphatic temperaments are less impressionable, less susceptible of being so enticed.

The sanguine temperament appears to be the more favorable to the activity of the genital organs, secreting a more abundant supply of semen, and more frequently by strong erections soliciting to copulation; the losses are also more easily repaired.

As to the nervous temperament, there is a confounding of the sexual organs with the mental, of which I shall hereafter speak.

It is not, then, in ages and temperaments that must be sought the real causes of venereal excesses and their dangers.

The ensemble of organs necessary to reproduction is composed of two very distinct systems; the one destined to the material accomplishment of the act; the other to receive the impulses and direct the acts as they are in progress. There usually exists a sufficiently exact harmony between them from the epoch of their evolution to that of their extinction, so that to the power and activity which they respectively enjoy it is quite right to attribute for a long time all the phenomena of a generative character to the exclusive influence of the sexual organs, more easy to understand than that of the brain.

However, I have already pointed out that the genital instinct advances frequently before the epoch of puberty, I must now add that the two systems have always an equal development, an equal activity. There remains to be seen what results from the preponderance of the one over the other.

There is nothing in the animal economy which presents so many variations as the sexual organs, under the double aspect of development and power. I have seen the most opposite cases. I have met with men who had from early life given themselves over to the most frightful masturbation, who have had many mistresses at a time even till they reached their sixtieth year, without their health having suffered, while others have suffered from nocturnal or diurnal pollutions of the most difficult nature from the slightest errors of youth.

Neither do these differences coincide in a constant manner with the exterior characters which announce the predominance of one of the elements which enter into the composition of all the organs, yet less with the development in size or muscular system ; thus with a temperament sanguine, lymphatic or nervous, with a constitution delicate or robust, the sexual organs present themselves under every shade of size, power and activity.

I shall hereafter treat on the indications one is able to receive from the development and conformation of the divers parts of the genital apparatus, for the appreciation of the virile power, for no single organ of the human economy presents such amazing differences in its functions in individuals of the same age and temperament. The condition the least exposed to excesses of an erotic kind is that in which the sexual organs predominate over the nervous organization. I have seen some young men of an extreme virile power who were never troubled except by their physical wants. They experienced frequent erections, importunate ones, but their imaginations rested cold. They gave themselves up to masturbation or copulation to get rid of an incommodity, thinking no more about it when the inconvenient erection was over, all their trouble to get rid of it and never feeling a passion for any woman: they were able to support these acts frequently without being incommoded, but they were never goaded to them by their imagination ; seduction and intrigue were not made for them. When they were pushed by the desire or stirred up by some orgie, they entered without repugnance into the worst places, and all was fish that came to their net. It was not in consequence of excesses that these men became invalids; those who came to me for advice were the victims of acquired disease of venereal character.

It is easy to conceive that opposite conditions are those which most actively lead to excess.

I need not here examine what is the seat of the organ which originates the sensations relative to generation, and which directs its acts ; it is sufficient to know that it exists, that its action precedes that of the sexual organs and predominates over them.

This preponderance of the genital instinct over the material instruments is usually announced early in life. We see infants interested in women, five, six, or even ten years before puberty, showing almost always the same sensibility for the rest of their lives to all which is able to provoke or recall erotic ideas, whether the impression comes from the organs of copulation or from the senses ; they remain the same, conserve a souvenir more keenly and more durable ; their imagination gloats over it; they turn and return in a hundred fashions ; these voluptuous images mingle with their gravest thoughts, interfere with all their meditations and follow them into the realms of sleep. They long for every woman they see, and are easily excited, but their virile power is not able to respond to the immensity of their desires. The sexual act fatigues them, enervates them, they feel it, but their senses carry them beyond their better judgment, and they give way to them as much as they can. They have no more power over their will than strangers : when they are worn out they make

the best of resolutions, which, upon regaining their strength
are always broken.

One of them, a doctor, full of imagination, said to me
that he felt then a burning heat in the occiput, accompanied
by pulsations, which augmented as the sensual desire became
stronger, until the moment when he yielded to the impulse.
As I knew what influence preconceived ideas might have on
his observations, I wished to verify the fact, and found after
repeated experiments, that the skin of the neck was swollen,
injected, and very hot; the ears participated, and I could
feel the pulsations.   Upon copulation this orgasm ceased, and
produced a relief which lasted seven or eight days, after
which the same congestion recommenced and increased until
it again overpowered the will and led to a repetition of the
amorous battle.   Facts so characteristic as these are doubtless.
rare, but rare as they are, they go to show how much this
brain organ has to do in exciting to venereal excesses.

When desire is only provoked by the presence of abundant
sperm, it is appeased as soon as the want felt is satisfied, and
renewed when the seminal loss is recuperated, there will then
be no real excess, if other causes do not determine the more
frequent repetition of the act.   But it is easily understood
what grave excesses are almost inevitable when the desire is
always in excess of the real want.

To this predominance of the genital instinct is frequently
joined a brilliant, active imagination, an exquisite sensibility,
a grand variety of ideas and creations.   The poetical temperaments which we call nervous, give the most seductive colors
to their recollections, embellishing them with imaginary
charms.   They create for themselves perfect beauty, ineffable
joy, and usually find the real far below the dreams of imag-

ination. Devoured by desire, but penetrated by a sense of weakness they unhappily rely upon themselves to find pleasures in harmony with their creations, and to enjoy all the sex at their pleasure, they revel in solitary delight with the woman they adore without the necessity of her presence.

If I add that this nervous predominance renders more impressionable the organs exposed to this abuse, to this excess, that their functions are easily perverted, it is easily conceived how much these unhappy persons are predisposed to involuntary seminal losses.

But it is not the organ of physical love alone which impels a man to pass beyond his real wants; there are other cerebral impulses which must be taken into consideration.

Self-conceit is perhaps the commonest cause of venereal excess. The man wishes, in this respect, to be thought above his fellows, and especially with his mistress. It is in her presence that he is proud of his physical power, of his intellectual superiority, of his social position; but above all he wishes to prove to her his virile strength, and it is generally those who have been the most slightly provided for in this direction who fear to have their weakness discovered.

This vain disposition is more excited still by that which rules with the woman under another form: she sees, in fact, in these repeated acts of love, the most incontestable proof of a violent affection, the most satisfying evidence of the power of her charms. She is too proud of it not to respond to it to the utmost of her power. These two sentiments, both born of vanity, excite both; they indulge in reciprocal demonstrations which are not founded on real wants, which are not even created by a real passion each for the other.

Young husbands who, without foresight, give themselves

up with all the heat of their temperament, endeavor to sustain the ardor of their first attack; they fear the suspicion of cooling down or going astray, and live to repent of their first imprudence—for their irritated organs are not in a condition to carry on for a long time the excesses with which they commenced.

If judgment is to be founded on details furnished by patients themselves, these venereal excesses are more frequently instigated by self-conceit than by the power of true love. I know all that such a blind, exclusive passion, concentrated on one subject, can do; it will not cause the impulses of which I speak, it will not even give the necessary energy to carry them out.

Let us here examine in detail a grave error generally admitted, that the influence of the generative organs is much greater, that the excitation of these organs is more lively, that this influence has more intensity during the period of puberty newly arrived than at other epochs of life; that it is more in the state of awakening or rest than during repose, and that it mounts to the highest degree during the consummation of the act. The natural consequence of these facts is that the greater the excitement of the genital organs during the act the stronger must be the impression which it causes. It may therefore be said that the faculty it has of being injurious is, all other things being equal, in direct ratio to the force and duration of the excitement which accompanies it.

This is all false reasoning. If the influence of the genital organs on the economy is proportioned to the energy of their activity, it does not follow that it must necessarily be injurious.

Everybody knows how favorable genital evolution is to the '

developement of all the organs, how much the general excitation which results therefrom is, above all, favorable to feeble constitutions, delicate health and lymphatic temperaments. There is not a doctor living who has not seen this crisis put an end to a whole crowd of chronical affections, before rebellious to all treatment; parents watch for it with impatience, in cases where the attentions of a medical man have seemed utterly powerless.

The comparison between the rest, and the state of repose of the genital organs is contrary to the conclusions. It is certainly true, that at this period the influence of these organs is incomparably greater, but is the general excitation of the whole economy from it harmful? Decidedly not, since the strength, the activity and the manly courage take on them at that period a new energy. And yet it is this terrible influ-

ence which it is endeavored to demonstrate is hurtful, that
the dangers of the act are in ratio to the degree of it. All
these conclusions are arrived at by starting out with the idea
that the venereal act is in itself wrong, and the excessive importance attached to the nervous outlay.

Whatever the case may be we will lay aside logical discussion, and see what facts are brought to bear out the view.

"Compare the two sexes," says one writer, "the female
presents less frequently the dangerous effects of venereal excess." Why this difference? Is it not because the genital
feeling with woman is less susceptible of exaltation, the venereal act causes them less fatigue? These propositions are
true, in a general way; but to what end does the statement
relative to the female tend? That her organs are not excited,
like those of man, by the stimulating presence of semen.
Why does the act of copulation cause her less fatigue? Precisely because she is not exposed to the spending, which is the
principal cause of the feebleness the man experiences. If I
were to insist on these delicate mysteries I could easily show
that with the woman, the absence even of this proof of the
act does not, as with man, deny the reality; and I might add
that, with her, the demonstrations provoked by the desire to
please, or the wish to deceive, cannot be told from the real
pleasure sometimes felt by them. The same writer says:
"They proceed less to the act than to the pretense of it; and
only have just enough desire to enable them not to refuse it.
Is it not a fact that it is both without desire or enjoyment that
a great number of women submit to the caresses of their husbands? Notwithstanding, let it be remarked, this indifference does not prevent them from becoming mothers; for the
sensual sensation is not with them, as with the man, an indis-

pensable condition to the generative work. Again, I ask, would public women exist at all if copulation had as enervating a power over woman as over man ? "

It will be seen here that no account is taken of the loss of semen which occurs with the man, and is finished by assimulating the contractions which necessarily accompany the ejaculation to the insignificant imitation of the act by the woman. What power can this have when it does not even produce a venereal sensation ? As to public women nobody ever supposes for a moment that they take the least part in the pleasures which they sell ; it would be a strange abuse of words to call the function which they practice *copulation*. Their part in this circumstance cannot be compared to that of the man's, since, on their side, the fact does not even exist, except in some special cases which they hold for their pleasure and not for their trade.

" One thing proved," says the same authority, " is that all which goes to give more force and prolong the duration of the sensations which accompany the sexual act renders it more fatiguing and is followed by greater disorder. No doubt when coition is reduced to its simplest form, that of a simple excretion of semen, it causes much less prejudice than when it takes place with great *eclat*. Thus commerce with public prostitutes, and generally with women who do not inspire ecstatic transports, will give less relaxation than those which are urged on by a violent passion. Some authors, however, think otherwise; but it is evident that these writers confound the state of the body with that of the mind. Assuredly when it is governed by a strong passion, the amorous heat will endure longer and satiety will be slower in arriving, but it does not follow that the body resists more. Decidedly not, only the attacks which it makes are less felt at the time, but they will develop themselves later, when the genital senses are silent and permit an accounting for the ravages which have been made.

Of course all these statements are qualified by the phrase, "All other things being equal." Are they really so? Is it possible to admit that copulation with a woman of the town will be as often repeated and as intensely enjoyed as with the object of an ardent passion? What is the impulse which is able to allay a most imperious need with a woman who can only inspire scorn, disgust, and inquietude on the part of probable disease?

All that can be concluded from the facts given by Dr. Deslandes is that the impassioned man is necessarily exposed to excesses which would never be committed in a state of indifference, and more strongly so if he has a repugnance. But this is not what the doctor set out to prove.

Immediately after the paragraph I have noticed, he adds: "One of the causes which makes masturbation more pernicious than copulation comes from the mental state which accompanies it." What leads the doctor to a conclusion so contrary to his premises? Yet the difference is enormous in the results, but is it the act most off-color which is the more dangerous? What contrast in effect as to the intensity of the passion, the vivacity of the enjoyment, and, above all, as to the height of the passion. Why, then, is the masturbator the more exhausted? Why does he experience a shock more profound, more durable? Is it because he is overpowered by the moral turpitude of the act? more or less of a regret that no more expansive sentiment excited his cerebral system?

Sad thoughts, bitter remembrances, grave preoccupations

have a similar influence on the act of copulation itself. Exercised under these debilitating circumstances it leaves the economy in a prolonged state of prostration. Gay emotions, affectionate, loving, favoring, on the contrary, a prompt reparation. Notwithstanding, in the first case the act is reduced to its simplest terms; in the second, on the contrary, accompanied by *very much more eclat*, following the expression used by the doctor. These facts are known to everybody and easy to explain; they prove that all the passions, expansive, excitant, diminish the debilitating effects of coition. Happy love must, by the same reasoning, produce the same results.

It is incontestable that a violent passion exposes to great excess; it is not less evident that this excess is dangerous, but that it is so as much as if committed, were that possible, with complete indifference, by the same individuals, will never be admitted by men who are able to judge by comparison. They will recall too well what degree of virility they have acquired on certain occasions, with what facility they have supported the expenditure of which they hardly thought themselves capable; and certainly these occasions were not when the acts were reduced to a simple excretion of sperm.

It is easily conceived, when one thinks of the matter, the favorable excitement which the entire economy receives from sentiments of joy, of pride, of shared happiness; when one knows the magic effect of the view of a beloved object, by the sound of her voice, by all which we can recall to our memories. Whoever has felt the irresistible, instantaneous influence which these sensations and these thoughts exercise on the organs of generation, must comprehend with what activity the semen is then secreted.

But Dr. Deslandes has distinguished the state of the mind

from that of the body. I shall point out that, *all other things being equal,* the moral condition—state of brain—most proper to exalt the genital senses, are also the most favorable to coition; it remains to be shown that the same is true of the body, that is of the sexual organs, or, to speak more exactly, the variable qualities of the semen.

It is a received fact that the intensity of the pleasure is proportioned to the degree of elaboration the sperm has attained before the accomplishment of the fact. The same individual, under the same moral conditions, with the same woman, will prove very different sensations, according as has been slowly secreted, long time retained or furnished precipitately and but recently placed in the reservoirs. Any one cannot fail to appreciate this by comparing the acts preceded by some days of repose with those which are rapidly succeeded by each other.

I have said *some days of repose,* because too long a continence may finish by involuntary seminal loss. The first act which succeeds to this long inaction is less energetic under all circumstances. But that even proves the rule.

Thus, the sensations are so much more lively as the sperm has been better elaborated, as it has remained longer in its reservoirs. The exaltation which its prolonged presence has determined may even be carried to producing an erotic state, approaching delirium, almost to temporary loss of reason. The pleasure loses its vivacity as soon as the sperm commences to lose its stimulating qualities and the act becomes more and more insignificant as the liquid is more aqueous. All patients who have had involuntary seminal losses from venereal excess have remarked this diminution of pleasure long before health was alarmingly deranged ; and I have

carefully noted this sad change, as the index most certain of
acts done imperfectly and without enjoyment.

In the same time that the sensation is blunted the erections are less complete, less prolonged, the spending is more
prompt—it even becomes so precipitate as to take place before
perfect penetration. The duration of the act is almost nothing, and it might almost be said of the whole transaction that
it is reduced to a simple excretion of semen; and it must be
added that it is less abundant, that the seminal liquor is aqueous, transparent, without odor and improper for fecundation.

Following the doctor's ideas, it is in similar insignificant
acts, that the nervous expenditure and the seminal loss must
produce less effect on the economy, and notwitstanding it is
just the contrary, however rare they may be these imperfect
acts are always followed by a profound and general lassitude
which is but slowly dissipated, sometimes lasting for twelve
or fourteen days. I have known so many of these cases that
it would be useless to enlarge on the subject.

If one incontestable proposition results from all the facts
which I have observed, it is that the diminution of pleasure
is the first sign which indicates to the imprudent, that they
have overstepped the limits of their real necessity, and that
the danger is augmented by the imperfection of the act.
Further, it is proved that the desire diminishes with the want,
with the chances of fecundation, and is less easy as it becomes
hurtful to the individual, less favorable to propagation ; were
it not so the human species would soon become extinct.

That which is here said of the venereal act proper, following the state of the fecundating fluid, is applicable to all seminal losses, however they may be caused.

In comparing them with themselves it is easy to demonstrate that they are so much more dangerous as they are indulged in with less energy and fainter pleasure.

I will not go over what I have already said of the effects of coition as compared with masturbation, since everybody is agreed on that subject; but I must point out that the same differences exist relative to involuntary seminal losses.

The same individual who repeats the venereal act many times in a night without inconvenience, is frequently exhausted by a single nocturnal pollution; he always finds the advantage of avoiding these involuntary losses by copulation. The normal excitement resulting from the sexual connection gives to the whole economy, and in particular to the genital organs, a healthy tone. The expenditure of strength is more easily replaced, and the ejaculatory organs become more opposed to the involuntary emission of sperm. On the contrary nocturnal pollutions relax the organs and gradually lead to diurnal and even fatal losses of the vital fluid.

CHAPTER XIII.

SEXUAL STARVATION AND OTHER EVILS.

It may be as well here to speak of what may be called sexual starvation ; for a natural and regular employment of the genitals is just as necessary to health as is bodily exercise of any other character. Nature herself proclaims this fact by giving to the celibant erotic dreams, voluptuous thoughts, involuntary emissions, and in extreme cases, in the male, a discharge somewhat similar to gonnorrhea, and in the female excessive whites, which going a stage farther will produce, in man, atrophy of the testicles and impotence, and, in the woman that most dreadful of all complaints, furor uterinus, when all modesty is thrown aside and the victim will openly solicit the embraces of friend or stranger, and which has no relief but in death. When a young man suffers from nocturnal pollutions, accompanied by lascivious dreams, by strong and long continued erections, and voluptuous sensations beyond his control, he should at once consult me, or some other physician who has made these matters a life-long study—who will be able to point out the only method of preventing such symptoms from degenerating into daily and dangerous losses of the seminal fluid.

It must be stated that nocturnal pollutions are always somewhat injurious, even when sexual connection is not possible. But the great question is to know when they are violently so, and when they become dangerous, and this can only be told by the experienced physician. If not too frequent, and if accompanied by erotic dreams, by strong erections, by intense pleasure, followed by satisfaction, comfort, and no feeling of weariness, they are probably not dangerously hurtful at first, but in the degree that these symptoms diminish, nocturnal pollutions become positively dangerous, especially when they take place without erection, without sensation.

A celebrated French surgeon gives the case of a wealthy bachelor who, from moral motives, refused to satisfy the wants of nature. At the happening of some slight domestic difficulty he fell into a state of derangement, with an inclination for suicide. He was cured by a priapism, during which he ejaculated his semen fourteen times in about as many hours, and perfect restoration followed. The following year the same causes produced the same effects, and a similar attempt of nature again cured him ; but he trusted too much to these fortuitous circumstances, and a third attack so reduced him that he had to undergo treatment for spermatorrhea.

While enforcing as much as possible the immense advantages of chaste habits, severe principles and moderate desires I must, as a physician, point out the dangers of an absolute and long continued deprivation of venereal pleasures.

Every one knows that young persons of both sexes endowed with very energetic organs cannot, without danger, support absolute continence without being either led into solitary vice or an excitement of the whole system which leads to affections of the brain, which may terminate in idiocy or erotic mania. I need not recall here the various symptoms or the crimes to which they lead. They are seen all round us every day.

The effects produced by the deprivation of sexual acts furnish the most certain signs of the force or of the weakness of the genital organs. If they are strong, this deprivation becomes a torture leading to the gravest abuses and to irregularities in all the functions.

> *Tormented with a vast desire,*
> *To solitude he flies,* .
> *His members rack'd with secret fire—*
> *He languishes and dies.*

If, on the other hand, the organs are weak and irritable, prolonged abstinence leads to nocturnal pollutions which pro-

duce a terrible effect, and frequently go beyond the power of
medicine to cure.

The modest maid conceals her woe
  Till nature's fount is dry,
Pinched features all too plainly show
  The woeful reason why.

She longs for Nature's greatest joy,
  Denied, she longs in vain,
Till secret vice her hours employ,
  And life's rich juices drain.

Perfect virtue is not in the nature of man, and it is only those who, when puberty arrives, hasten to marry and fully carry out the procreative function who can escape those perpetual temptations which surround those who resist and those regrets which follow when they fall into solitary vice.

Moral scruples are perfectly proper, but, unfortunately, nature does not respect them, and when those who have strictly obeyed what they think is the moral law would terminate the enforced chastity they find themselves impotent, not temporarily but permanently, not only with worthless women but with those whom they make their wives.

Let us for one moment consider the effects of absolute continence on the individual. If fatigue is injurious to all the organs, moderate exercise is necessary, and the genitals are not exempt from this general rule. It is not immediately after puberty that man arrives at his greatest vitality ; the different parts continue to develop for many years, and everything proves that moderate exercise favors development and is necessary to energy.

I need not multiply examples, but will relate in his own words the experience of a patient who consulted me about a year ago : "I am thirty-six years of age, of an ardent and nervous temperament. Five years ago I had the misfortune to lose my wife, and in the excess of my grief I swore I would never know another woman. I soon found out that I had overestimated my powers. Not to break my oath I had recourse to masturbation, not more than three or four times in the course of a year, and then I renounced that odious vice. I noticed that my chest was weakening, and that in addition to the nocturnal pollutions which I frequently had, that I voided semen whenever I went to stool. My losses are

very frequent, return every day, and my general health is suffering much. I have never had venereal disease of any kind."

Here was a clear case, perfectly sound organs, functions exercised regularly, but suddenly arrested. There had never before been involuntary losses, but they were induced by a cessation of regular copulation, and I found much difficulty in restoring the tone of the genital parts and the general health of the patient.

It is vaguely admitted by the general faculty that a prolonged inaction has the same effect on the genital organs as on any other, that it diminishes their energy and activity, and that absolute inaction leads to complete impotence; but it seems not to have been shown that the permanent action of the testicles, constant and unceasing, must have some outlet for the seed it manufactures.

As soon as the evolution of the genital organs commences, the testicles enter on their duties, and if the texture is not accidently destroyed they continue to secrete semen until a very advanced age. This being the case, it follows that in the absence of evacuation they must become, sooner or later, full, and finish by being distended in such a way that if the sperm is not emitted in a mass by natural means it must be got rid of some other way, and it is this which leads to many diseases, long continued and hard to cure.

As a doctor, the legal question and the theological theory are not my forte; I must, as a physician, say that a regular exercise of the genital organs is as necessary as that of brain, arms or legs; for not to exercise them is to lose entirely their proper functions, and when, by too prolonged inaction, parties about to marry fear that a too prolonged

inaction has impaired their virile power it should be their
first act to consult me or some other physician who has made
these complaints his special study.

CHAPTER XIV.

OF SECRET VICE WITH THE FEMALE SEX.

The female is exposed to the same danger in practicing
masturbation as the male, with many troubles to which the
man is not liable, as hysteria, vapors, cramps in the stomach

and back, while the continual accretion of ever-recurring
whites cause violent inflammations, aching pains, and are, in
their contagious quality, as dangerous as diseases acquired by
promiscuous intercourse. These lead to ulcerations of the
matrix, to lengthening and inflammation of the clitoris, to
uterine furor, which at times dethrones reason and places the
unhappy woman in the condition of the most lascivious animal
until an early death puts an end to her agony and infamy.

The face, that faithful mirror both of soul and body, is the
first to betray the interior derangement; plumpness and the
rosy hue, those greatest points of beauty, disappear; thinness,
sallow or leaden complexion and roughness of skin take their

place; the eyes lose their brightness, the lips their vermilion, the teeth their whiteness, and, finally, the whole figure receives a check and the elegant form of womanhood is wasted and gone. How often do we see girls plump and well made up to ten or even sixteen years of age fall little by little into a deformed or scraggy state, sometimes even to a crookedness of the spine, and a general weakness.

> *The rosy hue of youth decays—*
> *The budding bosom droops;*
> *And for the balance of her days*
> *The maiden limps and stoops.*
>
> *She charms no more, her beaux pass by,*
> *Some other girl to win;*
> *While she love's fountain has drained dry*
> *By voluntary sin.*

Not only do these things occur from mere manual pollution, but doctors have met with frightful maladies of the bladder among young girls, which were caused by their odious maneuvers, the instruments which they employed having slipped from their fingers and passed into the bladder, causing fearful agony and frequently death.

One symptom common to both sexes I name here, because it is more frequent with the female; it is the indifference which solitary vice leaves for the legitimate pleasures of the marriage bed, even while the desire and the powers are not lost, but merely misdirected. A woman who suffered in this way informed me that self-indulgence had so taken hold of her senses that she detested the legitimate means of enjoyment. I knew a young man, instructed in these abominations by a companion who experienced the same disgust at the commencement of his married life ; the agony of this situation, joined to the effects of this solitary vice threw him into a profound melancholy, which, under my care, was removed, and he was enabled to do his duty as a husband and rejoice as a father. '

A short time ago a young lady, a resident of this city, who, until eighteen years of age, had enjoyed the most robust health, fell into a fearfully feeble condition. Her strength decreased daily, all day long she was nervous and depressed, and her nights were without sleep, while an edematous eruption covered the skin. I was consulted by her parents, and after discovering that there was no derangement of the terms I suspected masturbation. The first question I asked her confirmed the suspicion, and her complexion made the fact certain. I pointed out to her the danger of the course she was pursuing, and with proper medical treatment soon made her recover her health.

Beyond masturbation or manual pollution there is another vice among women which has been called *clitoridienne,* and which is as old as the time of Sappho, and was popular among the Roman women, as we learn from ancient epigrams and satires.

One of Nature's freaks is to give to some women a half resemblance to a man, which, not understood, led to the belief in hermaphrodites. The size and shape of a part usually very small, caused the mistake, and the odious abuse of this part all the evil. Perhaps proud of this kind of resemblance, these imperfect men and women, in excess first attempted the virile function. The danger, however, is not less than in other methods of feminine abuse, and the results are as frightful. All these roads lead to exhaustion, to languor, to disease, to death. This last merits our attention, as it is, unfortunately, very common among American women of the wealthier class, and it is not difficult to point out a Lanfella or Medullina, who, like those Romans of olden time, so highly estimate this extra gift of Nature as to lead them to attempt to overcome the arbitrary distinctions of sex.

It is no uncommon thing to see women loving girls with all the passion of men, and even being insanely jealous of any attentions shown to them by the opposite sex.

The calamities which occur to women are similar in cause and in effect to those arising from the same cause in men. The fluid which they lose being less precious, less elaborated than the male semen, its loss may not act upon them so rapidly, but when they give themselves up to manual or clitorical excess, the nervous system being more feeble and the sex naturally given to spasmodic disorders, the action is equally hurtful.

With women as with men, however, enforced continence, either from moral or society motives, frequently produces the most serious disturbances of health. Dr. Tissot, in his work on Onanism, gives an account of a very robust widow of forty years, who had for a long time enjoyed the physical power of love and was suddenly deprived of her husband, fell into such violent hysterics that she lost the use of her senses; no remedies could be found for these hysterical fits except strong and continued friction of the genital organs which procured a convulsive trembling and an abundant ejaculation, followed by a recovery of her senses and a perfect calm. Another medical man reports a similar instance; that of a young woman who fell into the most violent paroxysms—choking, losing consciousness, and having a violent trembling with a reversal of the eyeballs. All other remedies being found useless, the doctor applied a hard plug to the genitals which produced an abundant spermatic evacuation followed by an immediate recovery of the senses.

Dr. Zindel, a celebrated physician in Basle, has published a work on the subject of celibacy among religious orders, in which he gives many examples of maladies produced by too strict a chastity. Among others, some relating to the dangers of entire continence among women whose temperaments do not fit them for a convent life ; they are so much the more victims of the fire which consumes them, from attempting to conceal it so religiously, and thus they fall into sadness, sleeplessness, disgust, wasting away, and nocturnal pollutions. He adds one observation which, perhaps, furnishes the strongest proof to which a coerced temperament has ever been exposed ; it is that of a young girl who, devoured by her amorous fire and preserving her soul pure, with an astonishing strength, was subject to pollutions even at the very time when she confessed her misfortune at the feet of a decrepid and disgusting old confessor.

"A young woman who marries an old husband," said one newly wedded, to her female friend, " had better be thrown in a river with a stone tied to her neck."

Of course it is among those who have been used to frequent emissions, and who have suspended them all at once, that we find the best defined cases of involuntary pollutions in the female. As far back as Galen these cases were known and recorded, for he speaks of a widow in whom the retention of the seminal fluid caused disease of the uterus; she had in her sleep movements of the loins, of the arms and legs, which were convulsive in their nature, and which were accompanied by an abundant emission of thick sperm, with the same sensation as in the act of copulation.

A celebrated opera-dancer in Paris was by accident wounded slightly in the left breast; the doctor ordered strict diet, and forbade the amorous pleasures to which she was much given. The third night of the privation to which she submitted she had a pollution, which returned the following and many nights, until she grew sensibly thinner, and suffered from fearful pains in the loins as long as she followed the surgeon's direction, who, being obstinate, bled and purged her in the true old style. Tired out and enfeebled, she neglected his advice, ceased to accept his remedies, returned to her feasts and her companion, and the weakness and its cause disappeared together.

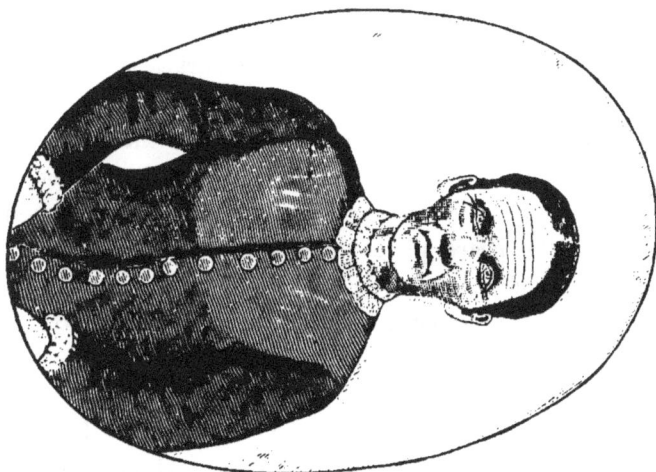

CHAPTER XV.

OF MALE AND FEMALE DISCHARGES NOT USUALLY CONSIDERED CONTAGIOUS.

Masturbation frequently brings on, in both sexes, a whitish glairy discharge, which has in man been called a simple gonorrhea, and with women is usually looked upon as merely a bad attack of leucorrhea, or whites, but it will be seen that they are very different and far more dangerous, as they weaken the body, induce various diseases, and may be conveyed from the man to the woman, or the woman to the man. Galen, who does not seem to have been acquainted with the virulent gonorrhea as now known from intercourse with diseased women of the town, describes simple gonorrhea as *an escape of semen without erection.* Many authors in all ages have spoken of it, and Moses, the most ancient of them all. In Hippocrates we have an example of a patient who had an involuntary escape of urine and semen combined. The great physician, Boerhaave, places this disease among the list of doubtful maladies, and says : "We read in some books of medicine that the semen is at times voided without the knowledge of him who loses it. But this malady must be very rare, and I have never known the seed to escape without some tickling ; it cannot be the true semen separated in the testicles and accumulated in the seminal vessels, although I have seen the liquor secreted by the prostrates so pass away." So far from this being true, Boerhaave was entirely wrong, for I have no class of patients so numerous, so dangerously afflicted and so difficult to cure as men and women whose seminal juices thus pass away—while I have no hesitation in saying that there are thousands of young men and women all around us who are suffering from this common disorder, feeling spiritless and weary without knowing what ails them. The dangers of this constant drain upon the fountain of life cannot be over-estimated. How can they be otherwise, when that which is the very essence of posterity, the very sign of vigor, the truest index of health, is slowly but surely oozing away? It is this which leads to consumption and an early grave myriads of our youths and maidens—and when once a weakness of the chest is noted, it is to a doctor who understands these things that the sufferer should apply. Actuarius, one of the wisest Arabian physicians who ever lived, says: "If the wasting of the seed goes on for some time without erection and without sensation, it necessarily produces consumption and death, because the most balsamic part of the humors and of the animal spirits are wasted and dissipated."

Most modern authors agree with the ancients. "All the body wastes," says Sennert, "and above all, the back; the sufferers become feeble, dry, pale; they languish; they have pains in the lungs and veins, and their eyes grow supernaturally brilliant or preternaturally dull." Even Boerhaave, in his later works, admits his error, and ranges this seminal gonorrhea, in both sexes, among the causes of paralysis, and admits that the discharge is true seed. "The paralysis," says he, "arising from seminal gonorrhea is incurable, because the body is entirely wasted away."

The evils which arise from these discharges when neglected are not confined to the individual—a man who suffers from these flows, although perfectly innocent of impure connection, may convey the same to his wife, who will suffer as much as though the disease were a true venereal affection, and the woman who suffers from long continued whites, either caused by too long a sexual starvation or from venereal excess, will be almost certain to affect her husband, who, ignorant of these facts, will of course attribute his misfortune to a lapse of conjugal fidelity on the part of his wife, and she, forever, will be under a cruel and unjust suspicion.

'Tis thus the innocent are shamed,
And husbands feel the pain
For which their guileless wives are blamed,
Whose words and oaths are vain.

The mother with her new-born child
Is looked upon with hate;
While she, with false suspicion wild,
Submits to cruel fate.

The Good Samaritan steps in,
Explains the harmless cause,
And thus again the wife may win
Her husband's fond applause.

Ne'er let suspicion gain a hold
Until the truth is known—
For married love is nugget gold,
And Virtue, Love's own throne.

MANHOOD—WOMANHOOD.

CHAPTER XVI.

DISEASES AFFECTING THE TESTICLES.

I have not, in the tolerably comprehensive catalogue already described, nearly exhausted the fearful calamities which arise from the practice of self-abuse. Among those which should be pointed out as a warning to masturbators, are diseases of the testicles which come in the wake of lonely abuse and inordinate sexual cohabitation. It is very rarely perfectly healthy testicles are found in persons who have practiced the one or indulged in the other. As amative desire and the power of obeying its calls depend upon the absolute sound conditions of the testicular glands, very many men go through life without ever having experienced the pleasurable orgasm to its fullest extent, while not infrequently the sexual instinct is entirely destroyed long before age would naturally have suppressed both desire and power of execution, and the man becomes useless when he ought really to be in the very zenith of his prime and sexual capability.

Among the commonest forms of derangement of the testicles may be placed a wasting of the actual substance as seen in the annexed plate, Fig. No. 1. Varicocele, which is a morbid enlargement of the vessels of the scrotum as in No. 2. With such a relaxed state of the testicle itself as is represented in Nos. 3 and 4, all of which essentially differ from the well developed and perfectly healthy organ as represented in No. 5.

Varicocele is usually accompanied by pains in the back and loins, local uneasiness, and a general feeling of weariness and lassitude.

When pressed by the fingers it gives to the examiner a sensation as though he were grasping a bundle of soft cords. It sometimes exists to such a degree as to resemble a rupture. In advanced stages of the disease, or disorganization, the epididymis becomes detached from the body of the testicle, and is plainly distinguishable by the finger. The result of all is, that a considerable diminution of sexual power takes place; and if means are not adopted to arrest a further break-up of the structure, the venereal appetite will subside altogether.

It destroys to a great extent the amative powers, and is frequently accompanied by a thickened condition of the prepuce, liable at the slightest disturbance to produce a perfect phymosis, which may require a surgical operation to remove. Of course, under these conditions, as no perfect erection can be obtained, penetration is impossible and procreation can never be the result of attempted coition.

Plato made a law that before marriage, to determine the fitness of the persons, the judges should see the young men who pretended to it, stark naked, and the women to the girdle only. The reason was this, that, in general, women were always ready to receive, and capable of receiving, but that it often happens differently with men.

If the abnormal waste be not promptly checked in the masturbator who has commenced involuntary emission, it will cause the genital organs to be arrested in their growth, imparting to them the appearance of perfect development, which is afterwards often followed by an atrophy or wasting away of these organs. These organic changes are attended with sharp, shooting pains in one or both testicles, extending up into the abdomen. Sometimes in aggravated cases, one of the testicles, generally the left one, becomes soft and flabby, and often both testicles are affected and gradually become soft and waste away. The sympathy existing between the genital organs and the mind, fully explains the despondency, the gloom and misery, the loss of memory, the frightful dreams, the hypochondria and inclination to commit suicide, and other evidences of mental disorder, by which the sufferers from the disease are distressed.

By Varicocele is understood a dilated and tortuous state of the spermatic cord. It generally occurs in the young, and is confined to the left side, because the left vein is unprovided with a valve where it enters the vena cava, or large vein, so that the blood is apt to accumulate in it and distend it, especially when it is brought to the parts by any excitement. Masturbation is the most frequent cause of this difficulty, caused by the rush of blood to those parts, thereby producing an undue amount of congestion, there being no means by which this congestion can relieve itself. In sexual intercourse with women, there is a spermatic fluid secreted by the female that lubricates the penis. This lubricating fluid relieves the congestion that is produced in the male sexual intercourse, and, thrown up against the female uterus and vaginal walls, relieves the congestion caused by a rush of blood to those parts during sexual intercourse.

Varicocele, in the male, is a very troublesome and annoying disease. The walls of the veins give way, become relaxed and distended, bulging out in places into little pouches, giving the vessels, when full of blood, a knotty appearance, which feels to the touch like a bunch of earth worms. The whole vein, in old cases, is dilated, enlarged, tortuous, cold and knotty. The disease is one very prevalent, although it has been known to exist for years without any serious results, but such cases are very rare. The majority of cases result in impotency and a wasting of the body of the organ, and by sympathy the whole body suffers. When any dragging sensation, heaviness of the testicle, or a feeling like that of many cords entangled can be discovered by handling, medical advice should at once be sought or incurable evils are likely to follow.

It is invariably seen in young men who have indulged to an excess in sensuality that the scrotum becomes relaxed, and this no longer bracing up the testicles, their constant pendant condition leads to a disintegration of the muscular tissues, and if continued self-abuse goes on the parts separate and varicocele ensues. Old-time doctors frequently resorted to an excision of a portion of the purse or scrotum, and instruments especially adapted for the operation were invented. But modern and more humane science has succeeded in a great measure, by bracing bandages and contractive treatment, to accomplish the same end without having recourse to such heroic measures. I have seen cases of this kind in middle age where the scrotum has been so relaxed as to reach to the middle of the thigh, and yet have succeeded, by constrictive treatment, in bringing up the corrugated skin to almost its abnormal condition, which Nature has aided by again contracting the supporting muscles of the testicles until a state of manhood has been secured and procreative coition has been carried on.

No. 1.

No. 3.

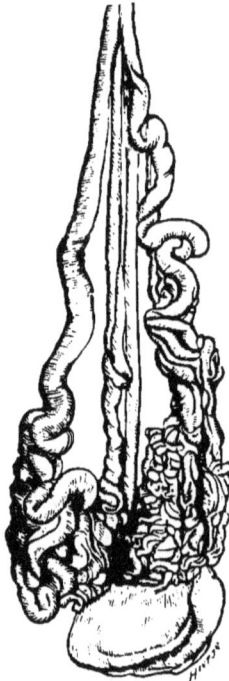

No. 2.

4.

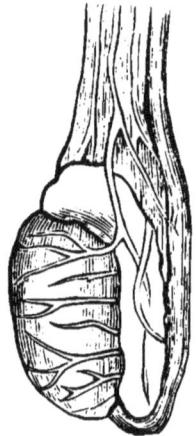

No. 5.

CHAPTER XVII.

"While the grass grows the steed dies" is a homely but true old proverb, and thousands of boys and girls become ruinously initiated into the practice of self-abuse before their parents or guardians think them old enough to be posted on the dangers of the twin vices of masturbation and mutual excesses, even if they ever are so warned. A knowledge of the sexual functions is just as necessary to the welfare of youth as any other knowledge, and, if we would have our children healthy in body as well as sound in mind, ten times more important. A man may get on and a woman answer all the needs of her life without much school education; but bodies once weakened by tampering with the secret parts are a burden to society and a curse to themselves.

Knowing this I shall now take the pains to go briefly over the whole ground and also give some general directions for the cure of involuntary emissions and partial or total impotence from masturbation and excess, cautioning my readers, however, not to place too much confidence upon self-treatment, but advising them to consult me or some other reputable physician who has made these diseases his special practice. To go to general practitioners is, I am sorry to say, too often waste of time and money.

While this is the case, every parent must know that it is wise to give the antidote. Tell your sons and your daughters the dangers.   Warn them to keep their hands away from their genital organs, for the slightest touch may awake sensations and arouse ideas which a lifetime cannot blot out.

> *In every place the evil lurks—*
> *At work, in school, at play*
> *The insiduous poison given, works*
> *Its health-destroying way.*

With boys the entire apparatus is so situated that friction on any portion will be sufficient to bring on the pleasurable feeling which may make him a confirmed masturbator. With girls the clitoris and the lesser lips are the parts which have the greatest sensibility, though the urethra with them is much more sensible than with the male, and in their childish ignorance comes in, with the clitoris, for titillation, and they have been known to force slate pencils, hair pins, radishes or other small things, backwards and forwards for purposes of excitation; these slipping from the fingers sometimes enter the bladder, causing inflammation, calculi and infinite suffering, if not death. .

It may generally be seen by examination if girls are in the habit of abusing themselves, as the clitoris becomes longer and hangs down, sometimes covering the mouth of the urethra, the inner lips from handling are also elongated and show themselves beyond the outer lips, the entrance to the vagina will be redder than usual and swollen, and if the hymen, sign of virginity, be not broken by the use of the finger or some other instrument used to obtain the coitive sensation, it will be found relaxed, and not closing the vagina so tightly as it should in virginal purity.

Both male and female are subjects to lascivious dreams during which the seminal fluid in the male and the lubricating fluid in the female are expended. Under the influence of unchaste thoughts, unsatisfied desires and erotic manipulation the glands secrete this fluid in an excessive degree, and it may be taken as a rule that a healthy, strictly virtuous and unabused female organ will never have any discharge of this kind until it is required to lubricate the male instrument of generation in coition.

As I have shown in the earlier part of this book, masturbation is a universal vice with civilized people, and it is a rare thing indeed to find a young man who has never indulged in it, while among young women it is much more general than might be supposed. From eight to sixteen is the general masturbating period, and the methods by which it is acquired are as numerous as the means by which it is carried on. It is called a solitary vice, but it is frequently carried on in companies; and I once was called into consultation with the mistress of a fashionable boarding school where eight girls from twelve to seventeen years of age used to masturbate each other.

Boys frequently find the various implements in the gymnasium serve their purpose, and will straddle the wooden horse, slide down the incline or even swing themselves from the pole until an emission takes place. This should be a caution to parents never to allow their boys to indulge in any gymnastic exercise likely to produce a determination of blood to the genital organs.

The earlier excesses by manual pollution are not so injurious to girls as to boys, and they are generally able for a long period to conceal the effects under the names of hysterical or

nervous excitement, but it unfits them for thoroughly enjoying the nuptial bed or bearing without risk, either healthy or
perfect children. Masturbation thus sets its unmistakable
seal upon the female sexual organs by enlarging and render-
ing callous the more sensitive parts, while we find in the
male a thinner and smaller penis than the natural development, the head or glans preternaturally large and the prepuce
also abnormally developed, the scrotum is relaxed and hangs
low, and the testicles are small and soft. When the vice has
been long carried on we find characteristic signs in the features. With women the muscles are flabby, the face pinched
and sallow, the eyes lose their luster and have dark circles
around them; the gait is weary and they seem afraid to look
any one square in the face. Sometimes unhealthy and disfig-
uring pimples break out upon the face, and this generally in
women of dark complexion. In males the face becomes pallid, the hands moist and clammy, the shoulders stoop and the
patient has a peculiar way, when sitting, of placing the hands
inside the thighs.

Similar results arise from inordinate sexual indulgence with
the opposite sex, and this leads to the most serious forms of
epilepsy and consumption. This, unfortunately, is not confined to individuals, but is constantly perpetuated, the defect-
ive seminal fluid gives to the fœtus the seeds of weakness,
and they only lie dormant until the proper conditions for
their bursting into disease are fulfilled. I will not say that
all, but it is a positive fact that very many, cases of pulmonary consumption may be traced to the sexual sins of father
or mother, or both. When this is not the case, it may be developed directly in young people from themselves indulging
in excessive masturbation. Of sixteen cases of consumption

of which I have taken careful note, eleven admitted that they had given themselves over to the pleasure of manual defilement from childhood till long after the arrival of puberty, and the others were children of parents who either showed by evident signs or admitted the fact that they were masturbators, or had indulged in long continued venereal excesses.

The amorous tendencies of consumption have long been noticed, but in my opinion they are the cause, and not the consequence, of phthisis. The great surgeon, Gall, relates the case of a consumptive lady, who, in her married life, had given way to uncontrolled and uncontrollable lasciviousness. She became consumptive at thirty, but did not restrain from indulging her libidinous desires. In fact, coition in every conceivable form, and with everything which could excite the greatest furor, grew with her complaint, and only two days before her death, while lying in a moribund condition, unable to move, or speak above a whisper, she begged of her husband to grant her as a dying favor, one more sexual embrace. Almost as destructive, if not so general among masturbators, is epilepsy, and in no way is the erotic tendency more shown than by the maneuvers of epileptic patients.

Dr. Baker, of an insane asylum in Cambridgeshire, England, attributes seven out of ten cases of chronic epilepsy in the male sex to the too frequent and violent excitation of the genital organs. Another physician gives the case of a female epileptic who had daily fits for three years, which were brought on by habits of masturbation, taught her when six years old. Her mind was constantly filled with lascivious ideas and dreams, ending in almost delirious delight from the exudation of juices, occurred every night.

There is very little doubt but that hysteria and epilepsy in young females, in ninety-nine cases out of a hundred, arise from sexual derangements, either from self-abuse or, what is quite as dangerous, sexual starvation. Young women of strong passions who refrain religiously from gratifying their instincts in any manner, frequently suffer untold agonies which are referred to any cause but the correct one, and unfortunately their timidity and bashfulness prevent them from consulting a doctor who has made these diseases his special care, or committing to him the exact state of their feelings. To such I would say, suffer no longer ; your desires and the results of suppressing them are in the order of nature, and all confidences are given in the strictest secrecy.

> *The good Samaritan is here,*
> *Why suffer secret woe ?*
> *But trust in him and have no fear ;*
> *He certain health will show.*

> *You 'll bless his name in after life,*
> *From sexual trouble free ;*
> *When you 're a happy, blooming wife.*
> *With infant on your knee.*

Those virgins who do not suffer from actual hysteria or palpitation frequently experience palpitation of the heart and vertigo accompanied by dimness of vision. The face becomes deadly pale, the pupils dilated, and the pulse almost ceases. These symptoms, if preceded by whites or followed by them, or if accompanied by a tingling and tickling sensation in the vagina or around the clitoris, should be attended to at once, as they are sure signs of sexual derangement.

But of all the dread effects of sexual abuse in either sex
the most terrible is insanity, and very many of the female
patients in our asylums have been brought to this state from
masturbation or brooding over desires which they dare not or
could not gratify. As the physician is not frequently taken
into implicit confidence, many cases of female insanity are
never understood, and, therefore, never properly treated. I
have made this subject my especial study, and am daily treating patients suffering from erotic mania. To the eye of the
scientific physician, who has made these diseases his lifetime
study there is no disguising the symptoms ; the pale complexion, the emaciated form, the nervous excitability or idiotic
stupor, the moist, clammy palm, the lack-lustre eye and the
averted gaze, all advertise the masturbator to the man of
science.

All cases of this kind require peculiar treatment, are extremely difficult to cure, and *must* be treated by the specialist.
Regular physicians as a rule place them among the incurables,
and imprisonment among raving madmen and helpless idiots
for life are the results of such opinions. My experience tells
a different tale. I have cured hundreds of such cases, and
when once I have succeeded in averting the recurring dangers
of involuntary nightly pollutions I never despair of my
patient.

Among the various forms of dementia among women, probably that of nymphomania is the most appalling. It may
arise from masturbation, from legitimate sexual intercourse
indulged immoderately, or from the desire for or sudden cessation of venereal exercises. It sometimes manifests itself in
full-blooded, healthy young women who have never fingered
their parts and who are ignorant of the actual sexual contact,

their burning desires without hope of being relieved so working upon their minds as to produce this terrible erotic madness in its most degrading form, when the victim will expose her secret parts to all comers and solicit every male to have connection with her.

The disease rarely occurs after twenty-five, and seldom before fifteen years of age. It is more frequently seen with blondes than with brunettes. When once developed all modesty ceases; lascivious pleasures are always sought whether alone or in company. The patient will excite herself to emit her vaginal liquor in a hundred different ways, and will frequently feign all sorts of diseases which will necessitate the medical man's examining and handling her genitals.

I had a case of a young lady, the daughter of wealthy parents, who unfortunately had been taught to masturbate by a female servant in the family. She became a slave to the habit, and when seventeen years of age threw off every mask of modesty, every attempt at concealment, and would masturbate at all hours when the desire came on. Although placed in the care of watchers and her hands secured, she would wriggle and twist about until she succeeded in producing an orgasm, at the same time indulging in the most obscene language. She had supplemented the vaginal ticklings by constantly handling her breasts until the nipples were as large as those of a matron, and at the slightest venereal idea they would stand out hard, firm and prominent as the virile organ of a man; in fact seemed to have the sensibility and erectile force of the clitoris. Her case was a prolonged and difficult one, but I succeeded in reducing the mania, bringing on normal action of the organs and a positive cure was effected by a marriage which her position and fortune secured, and she is

now a happy mother, a member of a church, and an ornament
to the society in which she moves. She lives far away from
any one who might have remembered her former state, and
her secret is safely locked in my bosom.

Satyriasis or chronic erection is a disease among males
somewhat similar to nymphomania, with females but much
rarer, and seldom seen except in mature age. Prolonged continence is frequently a cause of this complaint, and when present it makes the man as shameless in exposing his person and
gratifying his libidinous desires as is the girl afflicted with
nymphomania. He cannot see a woman without intense excitement, and will even masturbate in the presence of any
woman in whose company he may be. This disease is sometimes caused by taking dangerous provocatives to stir up dormant sensual feeling. These aphrodisiacs, as they are called,
should never be taken except under circumstances explained
by the physician and when compounded by him, as the care-
less use of cantharides, or Spanish fly, and similar drugs have
caused much misery and frequently death. When this disease
attacks a young man it leads to every kind of strange means
for allaying the intense amorous desire. Masturbation is not
sufficiently satisfying, but unnatural crimes and the insertion
of various articles into the fundament are common consequences. In its worst form it becomes absolute mania, and
leads to convulsions and death.

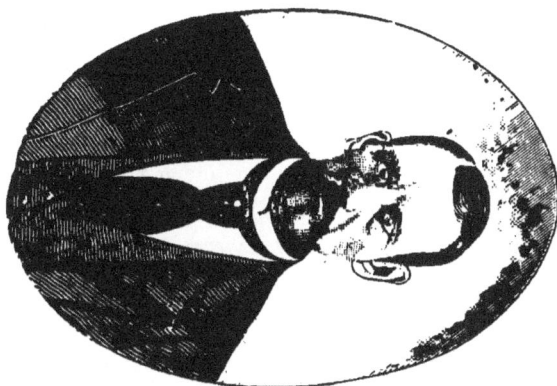

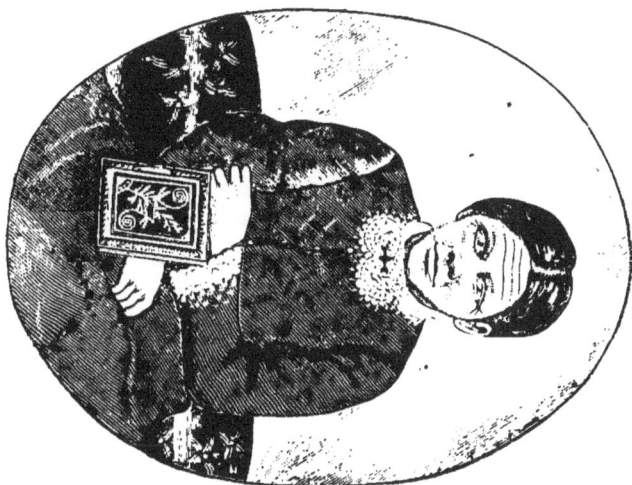

Sterility or impotence is another consequence of sexual abuse, masturbation or sexual starvation. Absolute and incurable impotence is very rare, for it must not be supposed that the inability to copulate makes a man impotent. If the seed be healthy and full of spermatazoons, it matters but little how it is conveyed to the female or how far up the vagina it may be injected. If the semen be left merely within the cleft formed by the inner lips the spermatazoons will find their way to the uterus. Women who have merely permitted the man to discharge his semen against, instead of forcing the penis through the hymen, have been known to conceive, and, though pregnant, were to all external signs still virgins, the membrane closing the vagina being still intact. It is a recorded case in the English books, that a nobleman who ardently desired an heir, and who was married to a young and beautiful wife, had a penis so malformed that its head was turned towards the testicles, and when in a state of erection it was like the handle of a pitcher, making penetration an impossibility. Dr. Graham, of "Celestial Bed" notoriety, was consulted; he had a syringe made with a surrounding space filled with warm water. The hand of the wife then manipulated her husband's penis until the seminal fluid was ejected into the syringe. This being kept at the natural heat she then conveyed by the syringe into her vaginal tube, and conception ensued ; in due time the welcome heir appearing. This Dr. Graham, although called a charlatan in his day by the old school doctors, and ridiculed by those who knew no better, was highly successful in all cases of a delicate nature, and many noble families enjoying titles, honors and estates to-day in England, would have been extinct had it not been for the wonderful success he had in curing the consequences of sexual excesses, secret pollution and impotence from libertinage among the nobility during the scandalous reigns of George IV. and William IV. He had a celestial bed, which was in those days considered miraculous in its effects, and many couples unable to consummate were rendered prolific under its canopy. I shall not explain to non-medical readers the means which were efficient, but I may state that the secret did not die with Dr. Graham. One of his methods for supplementing his medical and electric means of procuring a revival of manhood and a successful orgasm, was the exhibition of a beautiful woman in a complete state of nudity, illuminated by that effulgence now so well known, but then a secret with him, and Lady Hamilton, who was the mother of the great Nelson's daughter, and who was painted as Venus by the celebrated Barry, was his Goddess of Fecundity, whose appearance stirred up the sluggish blood of voluptuous and impaired aristocracy to the begetting of heirs to their estates.

It must be thoroughly understood that sexual starvation or entire abstinence from coition sometimes proves as dangerous and as prolific of diseases hard to cure as the greater amount of secret pollution. Among the most common and painful diseases arising from enforced continence is that of irritable testicle. How many young men lay the foundation of much after-agony and sometimes permanent impotence from prolonged excitement in toying with a woman who refuses the last favor and leaves the desire ungratified. The testicles will swell and irritable symptoms set in, which, if not scientifically treated as soon as felt may ruin the sufferer's manhood forever. Neuralgia of the testicles is rare among married men or masturbators, but is a common complaint with those who neglect reasonable exercise of the sexual function. This is so painful a disease that patients treated by doctors not specially posted in diseases of the genital organs have recommended and executed excision of the neuralgic testicle, which, though not preventing connection, usually does away with all chances of a family. Had these patients consulted one who had made such diseases almost his whole study, they would have been cured speedily and with no diminution of sexual vigor.

At other times, but usually from onanism or excessive coition, the neuralgia is induced at the neck of the bladder, when a constant desire to urinate is a leading feature ; and inflammation to some extent is always present.

Congestion and inflammation, which, if not properly attended to, frequently lead to chronic enlargement of the prostrate gland, is another thing to be dreaded from excessive seminal discharge, whether manual or in the natural way with woman. These are attended by pain in the peroneum and frequent desire to micturate, and should be attended to without delay.

The moral and religious questions which may arise in the discussion of the sexual problem are not the province of this work, which is strictly medical ; and Nature, it must be admitted, has fitted every organ in the body for some special work. Every artery, limb, muscle, vein and nerve has its duty. The fulfillment of all the functions are absolutely necessary to perfect health, and if this be neglected the whole body will suffer, while the individual function will be either impaired or destroyed. This is Nature's law, and she will be obeyed or punish disobedience. Never use an arm and it will wither, never move a joint and it will stiffen. Become thoroughly inert, and fatty degeneration, idiocy and death will result. Vegetables grown in the dark have no color, and

fishes in caves have no eyes. The sexual organs are not ex-
cepted from this general law. If they are not used they will
become useless. The organs of generation upon arriving at
puberty are intended to propagate the species, and if the call
of manhood and womanhood be neglected, the time will come
when the parts are unable to do their duty. When a woman
commences to menstruate, and a man's testicles come down
into the scrotum, they both must be employed in the duties
of replenishment, or they will become diseased and almost
useless members of the world's family. The longer after
puberty the marital duties are deferred the more uncertain,
weak and unsatisfying will the act of copulation become.
Remain continent till age creeps on and it is generally but
another word for impotence, and, should children be reared,
they will be either physically unhealthy or morally weak. Of
course, Nature does all she can to prevent humanity from
spoiling her work, and so warns young people of their duty
by giving them occasional spontaneous emissions, but if the
warning be not received and obeyed, it will become itself a
disease, causing misery and sexual ruin. A few times these
emissions may relieve plethora, and establish the proper conditions of the genitals, but long continued will produce pollutions, involuntary diurnal loss of semen and all the consequent
evils. The results of sexual starvation are among the most
difficult to cure, and are a class of complaints to which my
studies have for years been directed. I have every reason to
believe that I have saved hundreds from impotence, hysteria,
furor uterinus, delirium, consumption, insanity and death,
and my methods are moral in their nature, simple in their
form, and easy of application, without the slightest fear of
detection, so that the most nervous and bashful need not fear
to apply.

I am frequently consulted by men in whom the sexual passion has been gradually allowed to diminish by starving the
genital organs; in some cases where the parts have simply
become dormant from inaction, in others where a positive
decay—withering and drying up—have taken place, where
erections have ceased, and even lascivious dreams have failed
to produce an orgasm. There have been very few cases which
have not been cured, and in these there was a long-standing,
congenital, or accidental absence of either the apparatus, the
seed-secreting power, or such a malformation of the penis as
prevented insertion or at least the power of penetration. Of
course in such cases I have been candid and explicit, and

discouraged matrimony on any consideration; but in many cases where, by careful examination, I have discovered that though at the time total impotence was the condition, yet it was caused by a neglect of the organs and their being allowed to starve for want of due exercise, I have strongly recommended the patient to get married as soon as possible, even if he were incapable at first cohabitation to exercise the functions of a husband, knowing that if the act be not at first consummated, yet, under my Nervine process, it would not be long before manhood would return and the union be perfected, the marriage itself forming a very essential part of the cure, and far more likely to succeed than the only alternative, coition with a mercenary woman who gauged her endearments and caresses by the amount of payment she was to receive. I have known unhappy cases where, depending upon the advice of physicians who have not made these occult disorders their especial study, premature separations, on the plea of non-payment of conjugal dues, have been hurried on, when a Nervine treatment properly attended to would, in a few weeks, have removed all the difficulty and procreation would have been absolutely certain. In fact, to recapitulate, it is only where the testicles are absolutely wanting, the penis entirely gone, or such a malformation as defies surgery and precludes emission, that I have failed to make men fitted for the matrimonial bed. The testicles may not have descended, the penis may be reduced to a stump, or bent into a horseshoe shape by contraction of cicatrized scars from ulcerous sloughing, and yet I will guarantee a perfect cure and complete coition, and if the woman be healthy certain impregnation.

There is no more important office with the doctor than this, for it is one which causes untold anxiety, makes thousands unhappy, leads to melancholy, disappointment, madness and death.

Ye doubtful souls fresh courage take,
Lift up the doleful head,
My medicine shall yet fruitful make
Your barren marriage bed.

Do not despair thou victim of youthful excesses! Be not disheartened young man, who has suffered from venereal taint! Never give up the fort, ye who think your incapacity is permanent. Consult the author of this work and be hopeful. He has cured thousands and can cure you. Old men too should know that, if properly attended to, the recurrence of desire to copulate and power to erect will not cease till a very advanced period of life. If you have, in earlier years, abused your virile powers by secret pleasure or indulged to excess in amorous combat, that there is a sovereign remedy which will renew your forces and prolong your manhood ; or if, on the contrary, your penises are soft, inelastic and unable to erect themselves, the testicles apparently shrunk and dry from long continued abstinence, they may, without danger, be roused into activity, and, in the words of the holy book, you may, even in your old age, flourish like the green bay tree, and enjoy the inestimable blessing of conjugal congress till the patriarchal age.

CHAPTER XVIII.

ON PHYSICAL EVILS ARISING FROM EXCESS AND ABUSE.

It may appear a bold thing to state, but I think I could prove beyond any manner of question, that the greater number of diseases which afflict humanity are either directly or indirectly to be attributed to sexual abuse of some kind or other, are the result of hereditary taint, showing the existence of venereal disease in ancestors, excesses in immediate progenitors, congenitally tainted blood from syphilitic causes, or improper sexuality, sexual starvation, secret vice or want of proper sexual relations. I do not confine this statement to any sex or any age. Show me the man or woman, old or young, who is suffering from any chronic complaint, and I will show you either one whose parents have eaten sour grapes and the children's teeth have been set on edge, or one who has had either improper or no sexual relation, or been the victim of secret vice and youthful error. Of course I am well aware that this is a delicate question, and I will endeavor to handle it delicately, but will tell the truth so far as my years of experience, as a medical man directing his whole attention to diseases of the sexual organs and complaints arising from them, can do so. Properly considered, and written of in a proper way, no more valuable, no more necessary and no more modest subject can be treated of than the manner and method in which human nature is multiplied and perpetuated. The command, "Man, know thyself," is as imperative to-day as it was in the time of Solomon, and such a thing as a universal sound mind in a sound body will never be seen till men and women are taught to live sexually perfect lives.

The sexual intercourse that is in accordance with nature, and therefore the only natural and proper, is that which is based upon mutual love and desire, and that which ultimates in mutual pleasure and mutual benefit. First, there must be love, pure, unmingled affection ; second, perfect harmony of feeling in the sexual intercourse, then mutual forbearance, and finally mutual desire, culminating in reciprocal pleasure. Nothing like healthy offspring can possibly be expected where a woman sells herself for money, where a man marries not a woman, but an estate, or a big banking account, and where mutual love and desire exist, but where there is such a want of adaptation as to make mutual consummation at the same moment impossible.

If without these necessary conditions, and with these disease-breeding causes sexual intercourse be maintained for any length of time, disease and demoralization must ensue. The woman who submits to sexual intercourse against her wishes and desires, merely to gratify a husband's demands, virtually invites diseased offspring, commits slow suicide, and her husband is as much her murderer as though he strangled her in her bed.

But, bad as this is, it is worse where intercourse is carried on without regard to perfect and reciprocal consummation. What then must be the condition of things, when, as I know from a long experience and thousands of confidences placed in me both by husbands and wives, that a large proportion of married women suffer from this cause? This is the fruitful cause of scores of painful diseases, whites, terminating in a painful and contagious feminine gleet, diseases of the womb and ovaries, cancer, Bright's disease, phthysis, consumption, kidney difficulties, insanity and death.

It is a fact terrible to contemplate, but one which I as a medical man have to hear of every day, that very many women seldom or never experience any pleasure at all in the sexual act. Doctors know it, physicians time and again have acknowledged it in conversation with me; but unfortunately hypocrisy is as necessary in the medical as in any other profession, and they would lose their practice if they hinted at such unpopular notions among the parties among whom their practice for the most part lies.

Now I hold it a proved, positive, scientific fact, that it is impossible for a woman to remain in health under unnatural sexual relations, just as it would be for her to live upon a diet of arsenic, and utterly impossible for her under such conditions to produce, mentally and physically, sound offspring.

There is unfortunately a disease which has been for a long time getting more and more common, which is not alluded to by the physicians who have not made these matters their peculiar study, and it is to this that many of these cases may be referred—I mean paralysis of the clitoris. The woman in a perfectly healthy state should desire and enjoy copulation just as much or more than the man, and yet we find that hundreds of women merely submit to the embraces of their husbands that there may be peace in the family. This disease is, thank mercy, curable. The use of my Samaritan Nervine and other remedies will remove it, will establish healthy action in this member, and give to the woman as intense a sensation of bliss leading to mutual consummation, and when desired, healthy offspring, as the man himself can enjoy or desire to beget.

As in treating of these peculiar diseases arising from sexual abuse, but leaving the complaints immediately resulting from impure embraces for another and comprehensive work, I shall have to speak very much of the sexual organs in both sexes, and as a perfect knowledge of their formation, uses and requirements is absolutely necessary for every one who would, as Paul says, keep his members in honorable subjection, I shall, in as delicate a manner as possible, give a full description of the genital organs of both sexes. First of the organs of the males.

These are the testicles which produce the semen, the excretory passages, the penis and the erectile apparatus destined to carry the semen into the organs of the female.

Fig. 1.

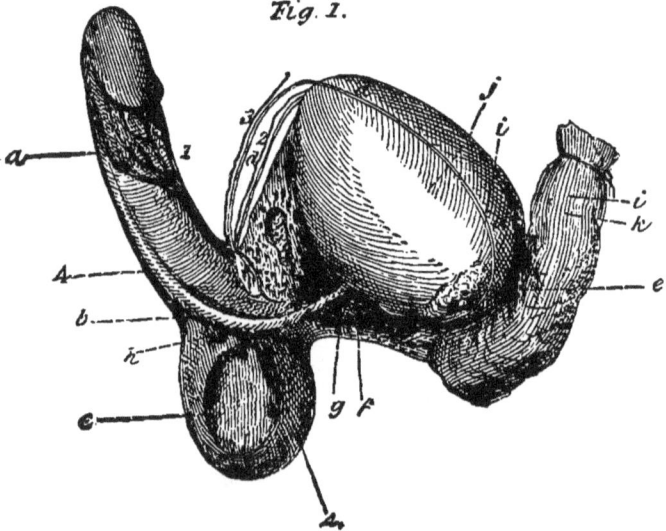

The male organs then are essentially composed of a gland (testicle) with the office of secreting the male element (semen)

channels for the purpose of carrying the semen to the exterior; such are the ejaculators, the urethral canal, etc.

Accessory glands destined to furnishing the products which when added to the semen modify its consistence and its essential qualities, giving it the proper physical property for expansion and fecundation, among these the chief are the seminal ducts, the prostrate and the Cowper glands.

Lastly an instrument of erection (penis and erector muscle) which under certain conditions acquires a sufficient rigidity to penetrate into the organs of the woman and carry there the semen secreted and modified by the preceding organs.

Fig. 2.

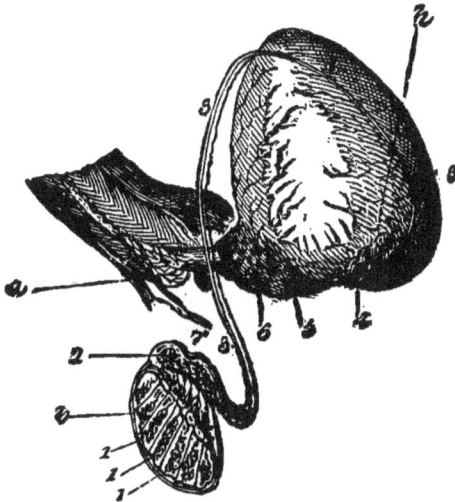

TESTICLES.

The testicles are two glandular bodies situated in the purse or sac, one on either side of the medial line. They are contained in an envelope formed by the skin and by several overlying coats of fibrous and muscular tissue. It is to this

envelope that we give the name (anatomically) of scrotum.
Among the coats which compose the scrotum we find :

1. The skin, remarkable for its brown color, so different
from that of the body, by its many wrinkles and by its long
and semi-transparent hair, by the presence of numerous sweat
glands and sebaceous reservoirs.

2. This skin is lined by a bed of pale muscular fiber, which
has a slowly contracting power, independent of the will, and
taking place under the action of cold, venereal orgasms or
direct excitement; it then diminishes the size of the scrotum,
increases the number of folds and raises the testicles nearer
to the base of the penis, near to the entrance to the inguinal
canal. In anatomy this bed of fiber is known as the *dartos*.
It forms in the center a separate nest in which each testicle is
found.

3. Deeper still is an envelope formed of muscular fiber,
which supplement the abdominal muscles, and are known as
cremators, because they hold the testicles suspended, and are
able by voluntary contractions to bring them up to the inguinal canal; these contractions take place whenever the anterior abdominal muscles become active. Finally the testicle
is immediately enveloped by a serous membrane, a closed
pocket without any perceivable aperture, which is the vaginal
tunic.

In healthy testicular secretion we find the spermatozoides,
which represent the fecundating elements of the semen, and
which may easily be seen by the aid of a moderately powerful
microscope in the semen when freshly ejaculated. They were
first observed by Louis Hamm, in 1677, and he communicated
his discovery to Loeuenhoeck, who, by investigation was led
to believe that they were true animalcula, similar to the infu-

soria, but modern science leads to the opinion that they were merely elements free and floating in the liquid, and that the faculty of motion which they appear to have is of the same character as that which is seen in some vibrating cellules.

Under a glass of from four to five hundred diameters, we find a head and a long tail; and in freshly voided semen the motions of these little creatures has all the rapidity of lightning, and so tenacious of the life they possess that Donné, in speaking of their remarkable power of resistance, says that they retain their form after boiling, and that they remain uninjured in putrid urine for an indefinite length of time. Another investigator, Henle, conceives spermatozoa to be possessed of an extraordinary amount of vitality, stating that he has seen motion taking place in tails separated and lying apart from the bodies; and Wagner noticed that the caudal end of the body was double, or forked, and occasionally two-headed. The semen is not altogether made up of the secretions by the testicles, but is mingled with juices from the seminal vessels, the prostrate gland, Cowper's glands and the mucus of the urethra, the testicles only furnishing about one-seventh of the entire mass, which, in a healthy, vigorous man, amounts to about half an ounce at each expulsion. In certain diseases this is largely increased, in others greatly diminished, and even after the loss of both testicles erections with emissions have occurred, but of course without any fecundating power. When we take all this into consideration we see how perfect must be the physical condition of the male when he expects his copulative efforts to produce a perfectly healthy offspring, and we shall later show that almost as perfect a condition must be present in the woman if she is to give to the world a really healthy child.

According to the celebrated chemist, Vauquelin, the human semen consists of—

Water, ...	90 parts.
Mucus, . . .	6 parts.
Phosphate of Lime, . .	3 parts.
Phosphate of Soda, . . .	1 part.
	100

The penis is chiefly formed of an erectile tissue, and it is to an accumulation of blood in the arteries and veins which causes the stiffening of the member under any kind of excitement acting upon the amorous propensities.

The genital apparatus of the female is not less complicated than that of the male; with her, in fact, we do not find a single gland destined to secrete a product which is analogous to the spermatozoon, not merely a copulative apparatus destined to facilitate the operation of copulation, but we find, also, the means intended to the preservation and to the development of the new being which is to result from the fusion of the two elements, male and female.

I shall enter fully into a description of these parts that my readers may thoroughly understand, as far as merely human creatures can, the great mystery of the reproduction of their species.

Let us take a glance, as a whole, at the numerous organs which go to form this apparatus. In the female cavity, between the bladder and the rectum, we find an organ which may be taken as the centre from which converge all the other parts. This is the matrix or uterus.

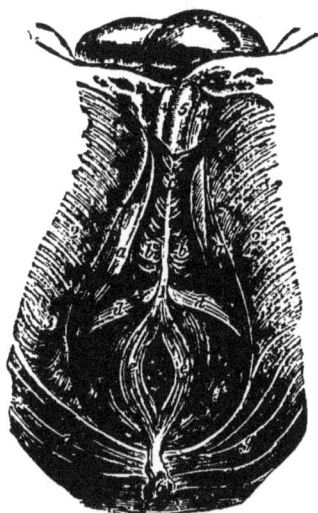

From this extend the uterine tubes, one on each side, to join the ovary, of which their office is to receive the product. In another place the matrix is continued at the lower end and to the front by a single mid-channel, which is called the vagina, and which receives the virile member and the semen of the male. The vagina opens to the exterior at the bottom of the pubes, surmounted by what is known as the Mount of Venus and by an orifice which, of itself, contains a series of organs, dependent from the skin and having varied functions, the greater and lesser lips to protect it, the glands to lubricate it and become the seat of those voluptuous sensations which provoke and accompany copulation, the principal one being the clitoris.

It would seem natural to commence our investigation of the female organs here, but we prefer making our account com-mence at the ovary, and follow by all its grades the ovum, fecundated or nonfecundated, until it arrives at the exterior; that is to say, we will accompany it from the ovaries to the fallopean tubes, to the womb, the vagina, and finally the vulva.

The matrix is kept in its position by two branches of the peritoneum, one on either side, and near their terminations are placed the ovaries, oval bodies very much resembling the small testicle. Almost the whole surface of the ovary is free, glistening and brilliant, and only covered by the epethelium of the peritoneum. The inferior terminus adheres and receives the vessels and the nerves for the supply of nutriment to the parts. When the blood accumulates here there occurs what is known as the catamenial period, and it becomes the breeding ground of the ovules, just as the testicles do of the spermatozoons. Examined with the microscope we find innumerable vessicles of minute size which are known as ovisacs or graafian cells. Each of these vessicles is calculated to contain an ovum, and as there are 600,000 of them in each ovary, it may be seen what an immense number of eggs, all liable to be impregnated, one female would produce if all the vessicles came to maturity. Need there be any wonder at twins? It seems that the wonder is that a woman ever bears a single child at one pregnancy; and this is a subject which, with all our investigations, we have never been able to explain to our satisfaction or in harmony with science.

At each monthly term one of these graafian vessels rapidly increase in size, and from being invisible to the naked eye it becomes as large as a small cherry. It is composed of an envelope filled with a transparent liquor in which floats a little monticule in the center of which may be perceived the ovule Thus the ovule appears to be the result of development of one of the minute grains seen in the graafian vessicle, just as we have seen the spermatozoon in the male organ.

The uterus, matrix, or womb as it is called in the mother tongue, is a hollow organ which above communicates with the fallopian tubes, and at its base with the vagina. Placed between the bladder and the rectum it is somewhat in the shape of a pear, flattened before and in the rear. Its length is about seven centimetres and its transverse diameter about three. It is composed of an upper triangular part known as the body of the womb, and the lower narrower portion called the neck. The neck of the womb is embraced by the upper extremity of the vagina which goes entirely round it.

The vagina is a muscular membraneous substance extending from the uterus to the external genital organs, and it has a length of from seven to eight centimetres. Its size is very variable; when in repose its sides touch and its entrance is nothing more than a longitudinal slit, but when it receives the virile member it accommodates itself to the size of the penis, presenting a dilatable cylindrical cavity, highly elastic, especially in the central portion.

The vagina is the essential organ of copulation with the female—its office to receive the penis of the male and into which is conveyed the ejaculated semen. It is in fact the portal of conception, and from that period closes to guard the mouth of the womb, except when opened by insertion or amorous excitement until it is used as the channel of expulsion for the product of the pregnancy, and it is through its channel that the newly created being enters into this world.

The external genital organs of the woman present themselves, when the thighs are close together, under the form of a hill or cuneiform protuberance, larger at the summit and losing itself in the perineum.   All this part is covered with hair, more or less long and curly, which almost entirely veils the delicate parts, which I will now attempt to describe.

If the thighs are widely separated it will be seen that the Mount of Venus is formed by the skin covering what an old writer terms "a goodly store of spongy fat."   From this extends downward a longitudinal fissure which is bordered by the greater lips.

In separating these will be found parallel to them two mucous folds of rosy tinted skin; these are the lesser lips.   These little lips unite at the upper extremity to embrace an organ more or less prominent and erectile, which is called the clitoris, and dividing them we shall see a moderately deep cavity which is called the vestibule of the vagina, at the bottom of which are placed two orifices, the mouth of the urethra or urinary passage above, and below and somewhat more retired the opening into the vagina.

The great lips are formed by a repleating, which, by its appearance and the peculiarities of its scructure, reminds us of the skin of the male scrotum.   Their external fronts, bulging and covered with hair, are separated by a ridge and furrow from the internal face of the thigh ; their internal faces are rosy, humid, sleek, and exceedingly sensitive.   Their upper extremities are lost in the Mount of Venus ; the posteriors by uniting at the base form a protuberance known as the fork, which separates the genital from the anal region. This fork is very delicate, and is easily ruptured when a woman suffers any violence ; it breaks, above all times during labor when the parts are not able to bear the enormous distension to which they are subjected.

The little lips form two mucous folds of a very variable

development; they are generally from eight millimetres to one centimetre in breadth; but with the women of certain races, as the Hottentots, they attain an extraordinary length, even to the passing beyond the outer and greater lips, and hanging down under the form of lappelles. Without arriving at any such proportions as these, it is not rare to find them very large among women of our own race. They adhere at the base to the internal bases of the greater lips and form a fringe to the vestibule of the vagina.

These little lips are covered by a moist, unctuous skin, very rich in nerve supply, from whence comes their exquisite sensibility, and in sebaceous glands similar to those which form the head of the penis. These glands seem more sensitive and more numerous in the immediate neighborhood of the clitoris and the vestibule of the vagina, giving birth to a cheesy substance similar to that found between the glans penis and the prepuce in the male, and of which the accumulation in the creases of the lips is not less irritating nor less disagreeable than that which at times leads to inflammation and ulceration in the male.

The clitoris shows an erectile tissue in all respects similar to that of the male penis. This little tubercle, scarcely seen or felt in a state of repose when covered by the fringe of the inner lips, under a state of excitement becomes engorged and juts out like a diminutive penis, and is terminated with a sort of gland having an indication of perforation, and covered with a moist skin very rich in little nipples—the termination of nerves of exquisite sensibility. Thus then the clitoris is with the woman the most sensible point at the time of voluptuous contact, and the erection which takes place during coition carries this sensibility to the highest degree, and makes it the principal organ of genital voluptuous sensation.

The vestibule is the cavity which is limited by the little lips, and, one high the other low, are found then the mouths of the urinary passage and the vagina.

The urinary exit is a little lineal or star-shaped orifice situated midway between the clitoris and the vagina. The two outlets in a woman are independent of each other until they reach the exterior orifices in the vestibule.

The inferior orifice is very tight relatively to the caliber of the rest of this canal. It is all so much the more so in the virgin, in whom it is greatly veiled by a peculiar membrane known as the hymen.

The hymen presents variable forms, which give the most diverse aspects to the entrance to the genital passage, and which are known as the half-moon, the horseshoe, the circular and the wedding-ring hymen.

Sometimes this membrane is imperforate, a fact not discovered until the arrival of puberty, when the menstrual flow being first established, a trifling surgical operation is necessary to permit the monthly flow to escape.

More frequently, however, the opening of the hymen is, during infancy, about the calibre of a goose quill; and at puberty large enough to admit the end of the little finger. At the first connection with the man, or on the introduction of any instrument equal in size to the penis, the hymen is ruptured ; its sides retire, and remain surrounding the vaginal entrance. They are called the myrtle-berries.

On each side of the vaginal orifice there exists an erectile body, of an ovoid form, called the bulb of the vagina. This organ is analogous to the bulb of the urethra in the male.

The bulb of the vagina is formed of a spongy tissue, with an erectile power like that of the man, and it is easy to comprehend that when the blood swells it how much it will compress the orifice of the vagina. So, by this action, added to that of the vaginal constrictors which embrace on each side the bulbs, and form a ring completely, the pressure on all sides becomes very considerable. This erection of the bulb, and this contraction of the sphincter, being strongly excited by copulation, closely squeezes the male penis and highly contributes to carry, to the most intense degree, the voluptuous sensations which accompany the act.

At the posterior extremities of the bulb are the glands of Bartholin, whose purpose is to secrete a limpid fluid, similar to the saliva which lubricates the entrance into the vagina. Sometimes under the influence of amorous excitement and contractions of the constrictive muscles of the female passage, this liquid is projected freely, even to the moistening of the hair and outer lips. Under the empire of voluptuous desire, especially when the parts are titillated, this liquid is secreted with great abundance, and floods the lips of the female organ in so characteristic a manner as to have led to the popular idea that women, as well as men, during the orgasm, have a seminal emission.

CHAPTER XIX.

THE COPULATIVE ACT.

Having thus carefully described the parts appropriate to each, and which shows how wonderfully we are made, what a complex machinery is constantly called into action for the purpose of procreating our species, and how intimately connected are the genitals with every portion of the human frame ; how the slightest accident to them, or the least disturbance in the regularity of their operations must be felt throughout the entire system, I shall now endeavor, in the most discreet manner possible, to explain the mechanical action of the act of copulation, as it will greatly facilitate our understanding the bearings of these parts and these actions upon those physical evils and serious disorders which are ever attendant upon either secret or social excesses, upon an extraordinary drain upon the vital powers and seminal fluid, whether caused by masturbation or inordinate venery, especially upon those diseases which, in ninety-nine cases out of a hundred, may be charged upon the abuse of the genital organs, or spring from hereditary causes, owing to such abuses. Among these, epilepsy, Bright's disease, tubercular consumption, rheumatic affections and impotence, are the most alarming and prevail to the greatest extent.

Physiologically, the act of coition is the one thing essential to the mutual approach and union of the sexes. It is the point of departure and the terminating station of all those physical and moral emotions which have been called LOVE.

The most absolute and tyrannical of all human passions is love, and its aim is made by all-powerful nature the continued reproduction of the species. How happy indeed is the union where the moral sense is as harmonious as that of the mere animal passion, when the souls unite with the body, and both being in a thoroughly sound condition, it may be then indeed considered a heavenly condition—a match made on earth, registered in Paradise, and blessed with the immediate sanction of Deity.

At the present time in our investigation of diseases consequent upon imperfections in the sexual organs and relations, it is the purely physiological view which we have to take. To make a study of love relative to the senses and in connection with the act which has for its object the reproduction of human beings.

In the venereal engagement the active role and the preliminary provocament among civilized people appertains to the male, though among some savage nations women think nothing of showing by the most unequivocal signs that they desire cohabitation. Modesty is not only the highest virtue but the greatest charm of a young woman. To render up a knowledge even of her concealed parts is for her such a sacrifice as to sometimes cause mental and physical disorders not easily allayed. She frequently, without intending it, and at other times by an innocent coquetry of which she but understands half the power, excites the desire of the man whom she prefers and to whom finally, with all the safeguards of the law, she yields up herself.

It is then the man who gives the signal of physical combination, and without entering in any unnecessary details as to the preliminaries, we will proceed to describe the method and the consequences.

The penis is in a state of erection; its introduction into the vagina is more or less easy; it is in all cases favored by the form of the gland which represents a cone at the summit truncated upon the upper side, in fact an exact fit for the vestibule of the vagina which in its cavity gives a fac-simile inversed of its formation. It is thus admirably adapted for directing the penis against the vaginal orifice. The moment the orifice of the vagina is cleared, the rubbing which arises calls into action the sensibility of the male organ, and the man, no longer master of himself but goaded on by an almost irresistible accession of pleasure, is led to multiply these sensations by provoking renewals of the contact which has excited them. He executes a series of movements which produce a lively friction of the gland against the folds of the vagina. These movements are still more passionate if the woman betrays a similar erotic ardor and assists by the heaving of her body the rapid action of the penis.

Absorbed by an indefinable sensation of extreme pleasure, the two sexes appear to live only for the carrying out of the act in which they are engaged. All their being is involved in it; the brain, the heart, the entire nervous system are aroused and excited, which alone would show to the thinking mind the extreme danger of tampering with such sensations or exceeding in the exercise of these natural and rational bounds.

As I said all the organism is combined in enhancing the effects, an extreme agitation moves the entire body, the heart beats with violence, the pulse is accelerated, the breathing becomes labored, panting and mingled with sighs ; the face is congested; a moisture supples all the limbs and accumulates in the form of perspiration in all the creases of the skin.

By the always increasing erection of the bulbs and the tighter contraction of the sphincter, the vaginal orifice embraces more closely still the base of the penis, and at the same time causes an ejection of the liquid from the Bartholin tubes which lubricates the genitals. Then the movements become more precipitate, more spasmodic. The erection arrives at its maximum with the man as with the woman, and when under this influence the sensibility is arrived at the highest level, at the glands of the penis and those of the clitoris, to that state which cannot possibly be exceeded, and at the moment when a supreme spasmodic contraction of the vaginal sphincter strongly squeezes the base of the penis the seminal vessels of the male contract, the muscles of the perineum and the urethra enter convulsively into action, and the emission of the semen, the ejaculation, is produced.

I have thus, as briefly as possible, described the typical physiological act of copulation in its natural and healthy accomplishment. In pursuit of the object of showing how these organs have the power, when abused, to cause mental and physical disorders which have not, at first appearance a venereal character, it is absolutely necessary to show how closely the nervous system is combined with the genital organs.

The relation of the nervous system with the genital apparatus are precisely of the same nature as those which exist between it and the salivary glands. The spinal marrow is the centre from which all these functions are ruled and its direct excitation calls into action the organs of generation.

It is thus that medical men explain why the extreme penalty of hanging very frequently causes an intense erection and frequently an ejaculation, for hanging compresses the superior portions of the spinal marrow and calls into action the direct nerves which det. .iine the erection of the penis and the excretion of semen.

More striking results are obtained from experiments on the lower animals, where the opportunity is found to experiment upon the inferior portion of the spinal cord in the neighborhood of the lumbar region, which many physicians hold to be the real genital centre. In vivisection on any female, wolf, dog or other, the irritation of this part causes very appreciable contraction of the uterus. If tried on the male similar effects are seen in the seminal vessels.

It has also been shown that electricity applied to this part of the spinal cord leads to erection and ejaculation.

Careful observation of certain human diseases lead us to the conclusion that there is in man a grand genital nervous centre of the same kind.

In maladies, attacking the inferior portion of the spinal marrow, there is at times produced priapism or an almost continual erection, and it is in this part that arise the nervous complaints which are caused by the excesses of which I am writing, and to which I have for years given undivided attention, and which has led to the almost universal appreciation of my Samaritan Nervine.

Every one will at once recognize the truth, from the pains felt in the small of the back after any kind of venereal excesses.

That there is also a strong reflex action follows as a matter of course, and it is thus that the abuse of the genital organs conveys to the spine that evil effect which is seen in momentary giddiness, dimness of sight, swimming in the head, a sense of falling, a swooning sensation and a limited loss of entire consciousness. When carried beyond this we have the patient in danger of epilepsy or some other form of mental as well as physical disease, which requires all the skill of a physician who has made such his study and who is able to properly diagnose the case from the symptoms described.

In a less and more pleasurable degree we find the reflex action at work ; when the perusal of an obscene book, the sight of an amorous print, the touching of the female person, arouses the genital passion. All these act upon the central nervous genital spinal system. With some past pleasures, with others the imagination excited by vague desires produce the same effect.

The new born trouble, the wants badly defined, which mark the youth just entering on puberty, have, without doubt, for their origin the organic work which is going on in the genital glands. It is highly probable that the nervous sensations born in the spermatic apparatus are transmitted by the nerves through the spinal marrow to the brain and that the gradual accumulation of semen in the seminal vessels causes erotic ideas in the mind as its influence extends to the brain.

The influence of the physical on the moral is here already defined, and the fact is incontestible, while the moral in its turn reacts upon the physical, as the nervous fibres emanating from the brain excite the genital centre of the lumbar region and represent thus the first links in a chain of reflex actions, which gives us a clew to the causes of many diseases otherwise obscure.

There are certain organs which, under the bearing of sympathetic connections, present stronger proofs of the theory still. Such is the nipple, and to prove how nearly this is connected with the genital function it is sufficient, without entering into details, to state that its titillation has a decided and immediate effect on the contractions of the uterus; to such a degree that a celebrated accoucheur has based on this fact a method of artificial accouchement; similar excitations, and even moral impressions are thus able, by a reflex mechanism, to exercise a grand influence on the monthly flow.

But of all the sensible surfaces, of which the excitement will lead to genital reflexes, the first in rank are the glands of the penis in the male and the clitoris in the female. It is thus the most intense sensations are produced by rubbing; in the nervous papilles of the gland where is placed the point of departure for those reflexes by which the venereal irritation is carried to the highest degree, by which the spongy organs erect themselves with the greatest intensity, and at last by which the emission of the seminal fluid is produced.

These sensations are so peculiar in their nature, so intense in their degree and so much predominate over any other individual feeling that physiologists have characterized it as a sixth sense.

It would, however, be an error so to do, for there is the direct opposite of that specific character presented by the five senses properly so called. The eye confines itself to the operation of seeing, the ear to the sensations of sound, whatever may be the state of the nervous centres in general, whilst the mucous surface of these glands only exhibit sensations which can be considered as genital, if the brain is disposed to receive in this special manner the irritation which acts upon them, and at all other times such irritations remain merely simple impressions of contact, which supports the theory of determining mental derangement in a great degree to the brain being overworked and underfed in the indulgence of solitary and sexual excesses.

CHAPTER XX.

IMMEDIATE EFFECTS OF THE GENITAL ACT.

The genital act produces at all times a considerable shock throughout the nervous system, and is at all times dangerous to those who are predisposed to cerebral congestions or to any particular nervous susceptibility, so that we see it is usually those who are most likely to suffer from even its moderate exercise who suffer from its abuse, as they are exactly the temperaments which are most freely led into these excesses, and they should lose no time in consulting me or some other physician who has made these diseases his special study, for who can tell where the reflex action will prove too strong for the nervous system and a serious lesion may take place, inducing one or the other of the terrible diseases, with a mention of which this section of my work commenced.

As it is imprudent for the intellectual man to go immediately from his food to his literary work, if it requires close mental attention, especially if such has been liberal, so I would advise such a period to be avoided for sacrificing on the altar of Venus. Hygienics may at least go so far in attempting to limit the indulgence, if it cannot now, as it formerly did, lay down laws and have them passed too, regulating the number of times husbands were to know their wives within certain periods.

Some medical men have laid it down as a rule that coition in the day-time is more enervating and more liable to lead to mental disease than the same amount taken at night, and that as the embracing of woman excessively exhausts the system, entire repose should be taken after the act, to repair by sleep and tranquillity the spirits which we have expended, instead of going about the ordinary occupations of the day. There are others who still more clearly define the proper period by placing it at daybreak : "For," they say, "we are physically and mentally in a more equal condition, our forces are not dissipated by the cares of the day, our stomach is neither loaded with food nor employed in the digestive process, and sleep has multiplied our spirits, rested our muscles and fortified our natural heat." This was the advice of Hippocrates, where he lays down the rules for the preservation of health, where he counsels work before eating or drinking, and sleep before Venus.

So far, his reasoning is fairly logical, but we soon arrive at a contradiction, for all physicians are of one accord, that the venereal act should not be entered on fasting, because no kind of work should be done by a hungry man. Other work exhausts and wearies the body, but the amorous act enervates it entirely. The stomach should be moderately full, and it is always advantageous to repair the waste and remove the fatigue by sleep, which is Nature's best restorer for all kinds of weariness.

Of course, no rules can be given on such a subject ; neither hours nor moments, nor day nor night, but only undertake the act when Nature's demands are imperative, when all the senses are in harmony, and when the accumulated semen and the proper conditions, with happy and undisturbed opportunity invite to its indulgence.

CHAPTER XXI.

NERVOUS DISEASES FROM EXCESS.

Now, having described the parts, shows how intimately connected they are with the mental and physical machinery of the whole body and mind, I will proceed to enumerate the nervous diseases caused by excesses, and point out to sufferers, or their friends, the best methods of restoration.

The most distressing malady to which my attention has been directed, and to the cure of which I have devoted incessant study, happily with what may almost be termed miraculous success, is epilepsy. This malady is induced by excesses, whether solitary or in the regular way of nature, and so insidiously makes its way by almost imperceptible degrees that the sufferer may be struck down without warning and become the victim of periodical fits for the balance of his existence unless the treatment be immediate, continued, and of the proper character. It is not at all a modern idea that epilepsy is the result of sexual abuse or excess, as to this cause it was assigned by the ancient physicians Galen, Paracelsus, Cœlius, Aurelian, and others, giving its origin and history. In old time it was known as the falling sickness, and the most extraordinary and absurd methods were resorted to for its cure. Of course they failed, and as many of the regular physicians to-day adhere to the same remedies it is no wonder that they are so unsuccessful in its treatment.

Epilepsy, or the falling sickness, is marked by the suddenness of its action, the fit coming on in a moment, with terrible convulsions and accompanied by clonic spasms, in which the muscles or muscular fibers contract and relax in quick succession, producing an appearance of intense suffering and terrible agitation.

The very action of a sufferer shows plainly enough how it has been produced, for the spasms are almost identical, though in a more intense degree, with that loss of consciousness and spasmodic agitation which take place after intense emotion from the expulsion of the semen. It may be, and generally is, preceded for some time by severe pains in the head immediately after an act either of masturbation or coition. These pains increase in intensity and duration until the ejaculation of the semen is preceded by a slight insensibility and followed by a convulsive motion in the extending muscles of the head and a swelling of the muscular glands of the throat. In fact slight epileptic attacks so frequently follow the venereal act that the ancient physician called every coition a brief fit of epilepsy, and, with highly susceptible persons, whether male or female, a regular attack of mitigated epilepsy follows the indulgence on every occasion. To these my Samaritan Nervine is both a preventive and a cure, as it so fortifies the nervous system that the crisis may come and go without any fear of these distressing symptoms. This nervous malady has various periods of approach, it may not come until the act has been some time consummated ; at other times it supervenes immediately after the excess which has provoked it. Esquiral gives one case, that of a female who became epileptic three days after the marriage ; but sexual abuses generally do their work insidiously, and slowly and thoroughly sap and weaken the whole system before attacking the citadel of the brain. Boys and girls may practice onanism

in early youth and be effectually checked before puberty, and
at that time, with the arrival of the seminal power in the
boy or the menstrual flow in the girl, epilepsy may be developed.

I knew one case where a boy who, on his sacred word, had
not practiced secret vice for nearly two years, was at fifteen
attacked with epilepsy. His attacks always came on with the
new moon and were of the most sudden character. He would
utter a loud cry, fall to the ground in strong convulsions, his
eyes became fixed, his teeth set, and after the fit the most
absolute prostration, physical and mental, generally remained
for from forty-eight to sixty hours. It was fully six months
before I dismissed him as perfectly cured. He is now twenty-four, and has never had a return of the fits.

Another of my cases was that of a girl who commenced
masturbating at three years of age, became epileptic at four,
suffered fearfully from convulsions, with total loss of mental
power, and when she was brought to me was but a shadow.
I took especial care to guard against a repetition of the self-
abuse; and, although she is now seven years of age, she has
had no recurrence of the fits, is stout and hearty, and, except-
ing a rather deficient memory, is all that a girl of her age can
be expected to be.

There is not the slightest doubt but epilepsy arises from
that condition of the spinal marrow of which I have already
spoken, and which is generally brought on by sexual excess.
Among the most terrible cases I have ever witnessed, was
that of a young and strong woman, but shattered by a series
of sexual excesses. She felt all at once her stomach fail her,
her head lose itself, her legs give way, her body sink, but by
a strong effort when the fits first came on, she would manage

to reach a sofa or a chair, and remain there until the attack passed over; as the disease gained ground she could no longer do this, but would fall suddenly to the earth wherever she might be, where she would remain, with a pale and convulsed face, the eyes half open and rolling, and the members cold and stiff as those of a corpse. She would remain in this condition for some minutes before she came to herself, or had sufficient power of speech to call any one to her aid. A high state of nervous excitement, attended with extreme bodily weakness, invariably followed, and it was many months before I managed to ameliorate her condition

With epileptics the secretion of the semen is much modified at the commencement of the disease, and when positive mania or paralysis ensues, both it and the genital desires are fearfully exaggerated. From this moment they give themselves up to all kinds of excess, but in the general run of cases this excitable period does not remain long, the genital functions become absolutely abolished, and they remain inert, leaving no impulses of an amorous character.

With women, the functions are equally deranged. At the onset menstruation is irregular, or altogether suppressed, and the hair on the head either falls off or becomes prematurely gray.

With men, as the spermatic secretions become less, there is also an almost total absence of spermatozoa in the semen, showing that impotence is a penalty inflicted for the reward of abuse; and with women, the cessation of the menses shows that they also become barren. It may be laid down as an infallible rule that the genital functions are finally abolished in both sexes, if proper advice and treatment be not sought in time.

A very perplexing symptom in epilepsy, arising from secret errors or sexual excess, is, that it may, after being cured, return under any great excitement, whether of a venereal or other character, unless the system is so thoroughly invigorated that all the nervous tendencies to undue activity are removed; thus I have seen the meeting with an old and unexpected friend, a shock from some sudden fright, and even the extraordinary delight at seeing the attractions of a show or a circus, bring on the fits after they had been absent for months. This shows that, however certain may be the remedy, it must not be hastily abandoned.

It would rationally be believed that the merest glimpse into the horrors of such a situation as this would be sufficient to deter the youth from solitary indulgence, the adult from sexual excess, and that the knowledge that it is, alas, too true, would make parents anxious that such knowledge should be given in the fullest manner to their offspring. But such is not the case. The doctors, as a rule, seem to ignore the danger, the clergy to hide their eyes from the moral Aceldama which exists around them, and parents fear to make known the dangers lest they should provoke the indulgence which creates them. To the young man and woman, when their passions are at their highest, and when they are about to indulge in illicit pleasures, I would shout, stop! halt! not one step further on the road of weakness, disease, misery and death. You are strong — would you be feeble? You are healthy—would you be diseased? You are sane—would you become the tenant of a madhouse? You have all your faculties—would you ruin them, and become an object of pity and disgust? You are in a position to make an honorable and blissful union; would you put yourself out of the pale of happy matrimony? You can beget or bear your species; would you become impotent, barren, without the power of perpetuating your name? Would you be ricketty when a child, epileptic as a youth, and die before you know the name of manhood or womanhood? If so, continue in this practice, and take no heed; but if you would avoid all these evils and live to a healthy old age, to see your grandchildren climbing your knees and your offspring strong and handsome, stop! stop at once, I say! One more sin, and it may be too late.

If, on the other hand, you have indulged to any degree, and feel the hand of the avenger upon you, the mark of the masturbating Cain gradually marking your brow; if you awake in the morning with the knowledge that your strength has departed from you in the night; if nervous tremors make unsteady your hand, and flushing at nothing raises the blood to your cheeks; if your pulse is uncertain, your head dizzy or your eye dim; if you feel that strength is not only gone, but that the spine is weak, that a dull pain across the loins or at the base of the brain is making itself a silent, yet unmistakeable witness to your excess, lose no time; a day, nay, almost an hour, may do incalculable mischief. Get the Samaritan Nervine at once, and, if possible, come and see me. There is balm in Gilead; there is a physician there. I have spent nights of study and days of research in making these things my own; in searching out Nature's hidden secrets, in robbing the herb of its juices, the weed of the fields and the prairies of their healing virtues; and I have compounded a remedy, a restorative, which I can hold up before high heaven and say to suffering humanity: thank God, while there is life there is hope.

In matters connected with venereal pleasures, the poet-physician, Dr. John Armstrong, in his "Art of Preserving Health" brings poetry to the aid of morality and virtue, and has the following beautiful lines upon the subject:

Is health your care, or luxury your aim,
Be temperate still; when Nature bids, obey;
Her wild, impatient sallies bear no curb;
But when the prurient habit of delight,
Or loose imagination, spurs you on
To deeds above your strength, impute it not
To Nature; Nature all compulsion hates.
Ah! let not luxury nor vain renown
Urge you to feats you well might sleep without,
To make what should be rapture a fatigue,
A tedious task; nor in the wanton arms
Of twining Lais melt your manhood down.
For from the colliquation of soft joys
How changed you rise! the ghost of what you was!
Languid and melancholy, and gaunt and wan;
Your veins exhausted and your nerves unstrung.
Spoiled of its balm and sprightly zest, the blood
Grows vapid phlegm; along the tender nerves
(To each slight impulse tremblingly awake)
A subtle fiend that mimics all the plagues,
Rapid and restless, springs from part to part.
The blooming honors of your youth are fallen;
Your vigor pines; your vital powers decay;
Diseases haunt you, and untimely age
Creeps on; unsocial, impotent and lewd.
Infatuate, impious epicene! to waste
The stores of pleasure, cheerfulness and health!

Infatuate all who make delight their trade,
And coy perdition every hour pursue.

There may have been a time in the history of medicine when a weakness approaching to impotence induced by sexual excess was looked upon as beyond cure, and when the sufferer from epilepsy brought on by self-abuse was considered a subject to be hidden away in the cells of some asylum as beyond relief, but fortunately that day has gone by, and I have no hesitation in saying that I have, in the whole course of my practice, not met with three cases which have been beyond the powers of my medicine and therapeutic treatment. In impotence, let the man have lost or preserved his venereal appetite, whether he has been able or not to satisfy the demand for copulation; whether he had diurnal pollutions or had not that present addition to his evils, and when he was not able to fully procreate or conquer the fit which came on whenever he tried, I have been fortunate to cure subjects who had suffered for years. They have not, it is true, recovered the generative faculty until first cured of an intense state of bodily and mental feebleness; but that once mastered I have restored their vigor, and they have proved virile husbands and happy fathers. In the female sex too, whether the woman tasted the pleasures of love or showed the utmost indifference to the sexual act, whether she received without suffering the caresses of her husband or was not able to endure them from pain almost insurmountable when she repulsed the conjugal act, from its being instantaneously disagreeable, and felt such constrictions in the genital apparatus as made conception impossible, with the added chagrin occasioned by this unwilling repugnance and this regretted barrenness, knowing herself to be the party to blame, I have never failed. I have, in fact, treated persons of both sexes who have been impotent or barren for five and even seven years, and have had the satisfaction to see them become fruitful after a youth of wasted energy and unproductive attempts to fulfill the law of nature.

CHAPTER XXII.

SELF—GUIDANCE AND MEDICAL TREATMENT.

The first absolute necessity is a full knowledge of the case; it is no use for either man or woman attempting to be cured under false pretenses, and an effort to deceive a doctor who knows what he is about is as absurd as would be the attempt to conceal your vices from your own conscience. He must know the cause or he cannot prescribe the remedy. In my confidence there is no danger, whatever your habits may have been, however strange, frequent, or outrageous the weakness to which you have given yourself up, tell it in all its details and then the whole system will be understood, where the evil is situated will be determined, and the cure insured and expedited.

For example, the treatment of a case arising from prolonged manual pollution would vary essentially from one caused by too great an indulgence in sexual intercourse, and with the female weakness caused by mere friction upon the exterior nerve centres, would be very different from what might be required when the orgasms had been brought on by penetration, let the instrument be what it might. Again it is absolutely necessary to know the condition of the male when in health, and what his average powers of endurance may have been, as it is to learn whether the female has, up to the time of her sickness been regular in her habits or habitually uncertain, with a thousand other particulars easily acquired when once confidence is established.

The frequency with which a man when he is in full possession of his virile powers is able to repeat the sexual act varies much with the individual, and what with one temperament and constitution might be but a slight excess would prove highly dangerous in another.

One thing, however, must be laid down as an imperative maxim, and that is that the best and even the only means for enjoying for a lengthened period the genital functions, is to use the greatest moderation. This is a hard lesson for young men to learn, but they will regret when too late if they do not acquire the lesson.

Unfortunately our young men and even old men are so little educated in sexual knowledge, and the common usage is so opposed to health and safety that under intense excitement, wantonly indulged in, the amorous assault is multiplied stroke upon stroke, and so prodigally carried on that more strength and semen are wasted in a single night than should, according to a true economy of health, last through a space of many weeks.

If the counsels of the physician and the learned are incapable of inspiring moderation, perhaps young people will listen to the words of the poet, who has said :

He who would long enjoy the married state
Must not repeat with love insatiate
The ardor of his amorous caresses.
It is the moderate man whom Fortune blesses
With health and offspring; but when frenzy fires
To oft repeated act, then Nature tires,
Obedient still to do her allotted task,
And dying to accomplish what you ask.
But if you're wise you will such ardor check,
Or soon, in soul and body, but a wreck
You'll drop into a self-dug early grave,
And on it might be grav'd, "TO PASSION'S SLAVE."

Young men should never be deceived by signs of a false vigor, and seek for an excuse in the urgency of the demand, for such intensity indicates rather a diseased state than an excess of vital force.

The frequency of erections is often a symptom of a morbid condition, of an incipient disease of the nervous centres, or the spinal marrow—the fore-runner of epilepsy, and are usually produced by a morbid condition of the brain, induced by reading lascivious books, or by constantly thinking on obscene subjects. This condition may lead to priapism, when there is a continual and painful erection, to satyriasis, the insatiable desire to coition, or of erotomania, which is love-melancholy ; to which subject Burton devotes a whole section of his "Anatomy of Melancholy." All these diseases in their incipient stages may be cured if taken and treated medically and hygienically, instead of attempting to satisfy them by repeated excesses, which must increase them, and finally render them incurable.

I cannot do better here than reproduce the words of the great practicing physician, Trosseau :

"If, with birds, and some of the mammalia, the ram, the bull, the stag, etc., the rapidity of coition, and the faculty of repeating at short intervals, is a normal condition, it is a sign of bad augury for men; for with us, to accomplish too rapidly, shows disease of some kind in the reproductive organs. In a normal condition it cannot be repeated, stroke upon stroke, with either complete pleasure or complete safety, and when a man boasts of his power to consummate eight or nine times within twenty-four hours, this exaggerated and false appearance of virility shows a morbid condition which is owing to some excitement of the spinal marrow, caused either by involuntary seminal loss or incontinence of urine, and I should at once expect to find incipient danger of epileptic attacks, unless the case is at once attended to, and the concealed inflammation removed."

The consequences become yet more terrible when the venereal abuse is produced by deceiving nature by onanism or masturbation. Every one has heard of, if he has not read, the sad pictures drawn by Tissot, and by other and more modern writers, who give accounts of the unhappy consequences of these secret vices, which are the most terrible agents in the destruction of health, and the ruin of mental faculty and moral virtue.

Continence, on the other hand, is not always without danger, or at least troublesome inconvenience, when it is too rigorously observed by a man whose temperament and powers lead him naturally to the exercise of the genital functions. Arrived at procreative maturity, man, says Dr. A. Mager, is drawn towards the female by an irresistible desire. All his desires seem to converge to this one point. "It is a true crisis, both of the mind and the body, of which marriage is the only natural and moral solution, while such is also the

most favorable to a healthy condition, both of the individual and of society. If copulation is not absolutely indispensable to the preservation of health, it at least exalts life, both for male and female, and is especially the agent in procuring the plenitude of charms for woman, who seldom exhibits her perfect beauty until after marriage. Our knowledge of physiology will not permit us to acknowledge that with man the re-absorption of the semen and its return into the blood are favorable to the vigor of the muscles or the brightness of the intellect. Speaking from a medical standpoint, athletes make a mistake who thus husband their resources in the hope of becoming more powerful, as do scholars who condemn themselves to absolute continence in the interests of their study and their genius."

"It is the abuse and not the moderate and physiological use of commerce with the opposite sex which carries with it a fatal shock to physical energy and intellectual power. The accumulation in the secretive organs of generation of the pro-creative fluid is at times a real danger, needing the advice of a physician; it produces a state of sensibility and of excitation peculiarly dangerous to the entire nervous system."

It is true that under these circumstances nature attempts relief by nocturnal pollutions, by which she evacuates the tes-ticles and seminal vessels; but this spontaneous evacuation constitutes in itself a danger and must not be considered as a true physiological function. If nocturnal emissions accom-panied by pleasure occur at more than very rare intervals, the sufferer from them should at once consult me or some other able physician, and if such occur at all without pleasurable symptoms there is absolute danger and no time should be lost.

With those whose temperament is ardent and whose ideas seem naturally to run to lascivious dreams, an imperious need of medical advice exists, for with them the nocturnal pollutions will become more and more frequent until they will degenerate into diurnal pollutions and so prove the cause of a rapid wasting away.

With men of a colder nature who are able to concentrate their minds on serious objects, on abstract studies, the pollu-tions will be more rare; but even such cases should be looked after, as occasional emissions make a bad impression on the mental state.

"It is with sorrow," says the great physician Diday, "that I see elevated to the rank of a natural and harmless function these seminal losses, of which men have a fear and a disgust, reproaching themselves for an involuntary act which always leaves after it physical or mental prostration. Compare this feeling with the moral state and pure joy to the instinctive pride which follows, notwithstanding the sweet languor of the first few minutes after cohabitation with a loved wife, and say if, after as before, Nature has not designated sufficiently clearly that which pleases and that which offends her."

In the condition where moderate and regular lawful copulation is used the quantity of semen ejaculated varies from one to six grammes (about 15.438 to 92.628 grains), but here we find a great variation of quantity in individuals, and even with the same individual at different periods and under different circumstances, as I have elsewhere explained; these variations may be looked on as in the proportion of 1 to 8.

The emitted semen is a complex mixture of all the secretions of the male organs. This excretion is white or slightly amber; its character is mucilaginous, heavier than water, in which it floats in the form of opalescent flakes.

Its odor is very peculiar—it is the *spermatic odor*. Some flowers, those of the chestnut and the hemp, emit a similar one from their masculine blossoms. Its taste is slightly salt. Although immediately upon emission it is of a thick and gummy consistency, it is not long before it liquifies completely if not exposed to rapid evaporation. In other cases it dries and gives on the linen stains, which cannot be mistaken, of a yellowish hue. This circumstance carefully attended to will give to parents and teachers an almost infallible guide by which, with a little care, they can discover whether children are indulging in stolen pleasures or are the victims of nocturnal pollutions.

So very mysterious, so very peculiar, so little understood, and yet so terribly frequent is an epileptic condition, that it is only by considering the entire economy of the sexual organs and the use and abuse of them, that the physician can form an opinion as to whether it is to be traced to their account. The fearful nature of the disorder, the strange and violent symptoms which characterize it and seem to remove it from the domain of ordinary disease, in ancient times led it to be considered a sort of demoniacal possession, and in Hippocrates we find it described as the "fatal disease." That it was known in the time of our Savior, and then considered as something more than a mere bodily complaint, is seen from the very accurate manner in which St. Luke, himself a physician, describes an epileptic seizure in the thirty-ninth verse of the second chapter of his gospel. "And lo, a spirit taketh him and he suddenly crieth out, and it teareth him that he foamed again, and bruising him hardly departeth from him." Too frequently that spirit is the spirit of unbridled lust, of erotic disease and secret abuse, and statistics prove that it is to these causes a large number of epileptic cases are due."

That eminent English physician Dr. Sieveking, of London, in his treatise on epileptiform seizures, says:

"The relation between the sexual organs and epilepsy is one that deserves our especial attention, since it appears undoubted that the physiological evolution of these organs, no less than certain morbid states, are found so frequently associated with epilepsy as to justify the inference that they may stand in closer relation than one of mere coincidence." There is no doubt of this, but I do not think the doctor goes far enough, for my practice which has been, in this direction, very extensive goes to prove that in the greater majority of cases the epileptic seizure may be directly traced to some abuse or other of the genital organs. At what period of life, for instance, does epilepsy most frequently intervene? At the time of puberty or during the early days of erotic passion. The physiological character of puberty is the development of the sexual powers, and anything which unduly stimulates or interferes with that development gives rise to a violent reaction, so that in the treatment of epilepsy, whether in the male or female sex, an inquiry into the state of the sexual organs is the most important part of the investigation. So entirely different, however, are its causes that we look for its production in the male by venereal indulgence or solitary abuse, and in the female from continence and a consequent undue excitement of the nervous system.

An ancient medical proverb says, " coitus brevis epilepsia est;" that is, accelerated copulation is epilepsy. I have known cases where an epileptic fit has followed immediately upon copulation, and with females I have known marriage cure it at once and forever. It is a well known fact that parties who have been cured in hospitals where they had no chance of sexual intercourse, have been siezed again as soon as they were outside and began to follow again their sexual impulses. Dr. Delasauve refers to one man who on five occasions was allowed to return to his wife, and came back each time, after a few weeks, with an aggravated attack of the malady heightened by maniacal delirium from legitimately exercising his matrimonial rights.

It is generally by enfeebling the system with sexual indulgence that epilepsy is induced, and it has been observed that in epileptics the sexual feeling is so strong that the temptation to vicious indulgence is almost beyond control. Masturbation, in both boys and girls, is a fruitful cause of complaint, and should always be suspected. When young females suffer from sexual irritation caused by leucorrheal discharge and severe itching, manual pollution is frequently induced, and this, carried to the slightest excess, is followed by epileptic seizure, and immediate medical attendance should be secured to counteract the effects upon the uterus and the ovaries.

In a person guilty of masturbation we generally find a downcast expression, an unwillingness to meet the eye ; a large, sluggish pupil ; a pale, livid hue and languid circulation, and all these signs are equally indicative of epileptic tendency.

I have met with but very few cases where close questioning did not disclose the fact that the sexual system had been greatly excited by either recent or long-continued, if abandoned, masturbation ; and many of them, having given it up, were troubled with frequent seminal emissions, which were doubtless instrumental in bringing on the epileptic fits, and which cases are by far the most difficult to cure ; therefore, I would have sufferers consult me at once, as no one can tell the fearful consequences of postponing what in the end is inevitable, if they would escape a madhouse or a grave. Nothing in the world can be gained by putting off a positive necessary medical examination and treatment.

I will quote one case in illustration. Mr. Y——, a young gentleman twenty-three years of age, of delicate constitution, who had been subject to epilepsy for about two years, preceded by one of those peculiar sensations known as forerunners of the disease, which commenced in the little finger of the right hand and mounted up into the head, after which general spasms of all the extremities, with unconsciousness,

follow. · The attacks occur alternately in the evening and the morning ; and he had about fifteen severe fits altogether, without reckoning spasms not producing forgetfulness. He attributes his attacks to masturbation, which, however, he has entirely quit. He continues, however, to have very frequent involuntary emissions, which are always followed by a seizure. Recently they have grown more numerous, and he finds that he has attacks in his sleep, from discovering signs of the discharge in the morning, and from experiencing all those feelings of depression and exhaustion which characterize the conclusion of fits when in the waking state. I happily relieved him from this condition within three months, and he is, to-day, as free from involuntary emissions and epileptic seizures as he was before he commenced the baneful practice of masturbation.

With females, epilepsy, at and after puberty, is frequently intimately connected with derangement of the menstrual flow, but it is extremely difficult to determine exactly what influence sexual abuse has had on the attacks, as women will not expose to the medical man their solitary indulgences, but it is very seldom the medical man makes a mistake who takes it for granted that evil practices of some kind are at the bottom of the predisposing causes. One thing is certain, you never find in the female sex, or very rarely indeed, an epileptic condition without irregularity of some of the sexual functions, or disease of the genital organs, and the first thing to do is to regulate these things before attempting purely anti-epileptic treatment. Frequently with the cure of the sexual difficulty the epileptic state will entirely disappear, and to become sound sexually is to become mentally well ; in others, though the uterine malady may be cured, the epilepsy will persist.

A great deal has been brought forward by doctors about
marriage in cases of epilepsy. That it stops the masturbating
habit in males and relieves many sexual difficulties in women
I must allow ; but it is a further fact that the conjugal em
brace itself may become a cause of epilepsy, and, if parents
have been epileptic previous to marriage, there is great danger
of their offspring being so too, unless they place themselves
under such treatment as will radically remove the epileptic
taint from their system, and which I flatter myself I have
discovered an infallible method of doing. The morbid
taint may remain hidden for a long period and reappear at
any time either in the husband, the wife or the children, so
that whenever there is a suspicion it is wise to seek advice,
for what an agony to a conjugal partner must it be after, perhaps, years of wedded bliss to find out all at once that your
companion is an epileptic.

I should recommend any one, male or female, who has at
any time suffered from symptoms indicating an epileptic condition to consult me before entering into the married state,
when I would take into consideration the entire story and
aspects of the case before giving either advice or treatment
and secure my patient from perhaps a life of agony and re-
morse at the thoughts of having been the parent of offspring
cursed with hereditary epilepsy.

Another frequent cause of epilepsy is a syphilitic condition
or aggravated gleet with stricture; but of these diseases which
are foreign to my present purpose I shall treat in another and
forthcoming work.

I cannot omit one symptom which should be carefully observed. It is that of spasmodic movements just at the point
of going to sleep, or a sudden starting out of a sound slumber

with some sense of danger and oppression, a sudden convulsion making the whole body quiver from head to heel. These symptoms show a highly nervous condition which, if not attended to, may terminate in positive and unmistakable epilepsy.

Seminal discharges during the night depend in a high degree upon the influence exercised upon the spinal cord by the hardness or softness of the bed, and I have already shown how close an affinity there is between involuntary seminal emissions and epilepsy.

There are some peculiar feature connected with this disease which no doctor is able to explain, such as the woman mentioned by La Motte, who was eight times pregnant; five of her children were girls, three were boys. Every time she was pregnant with boys she had epileptic fits, but such did not occur when she carried a female child. With children and also frequently with adult males a strong erection of the penis accompanies epileptic seizure, and involuntary passing of the urine is very characteristic.

No disease afflicting humanity has given the medical faculty more trouble than epilepsy; its cause, its seat, its course, its diagnosis and its cure have all been enigmas which they have in vain tried to solve. The old physicians attributed its attacks to the influence of the moon; others would have it to possession by evil spirits. Even the names given to it show how utterly at a loss writers on diseases were to give it even a characteristic nomenclature. It was called *morbus sacer*, because it was to be cured by divine, not human means; it was also known as *comitialis*, because it was frequently seen in the crowded assemblies of the Romans, in the amphitheatre when the passions of the people were aroused. Another name was

Herculeus, because Hercules is said to have been afflicted
with it; and until very recent times it was known as *caducus*
or the falling sickness, which merely described its action and
not its nature.

Just as numerous and absurd were the supposed cures for
the malady ; the eating of tame cats, the brains of vultures,
the raw heart of a sea gull, fresh human blood drank fasting,
the human liver fried, also the liver of a weasel, the pounded
skull of an ass, the ashes of cloths saturated in the blood of
gladiators, rubbing with an ointment made of chameleons
boiled in oil ; placing two small pebbles, one black the other
white, found in the maws of young swallows, on the patient
during the fit, drinking the warm blood of gladiators slain in
the amphitheatre, the human skull rasped and beaten in a
mortar, with the essence of black cherries, have all been seriously prescribed and faithfully taken by epileptic sufferers.

Bad as these remedies were, modern physicians out-did
them by attempting to cure epilepsy by heroic blood-letting,
and by the actual cautery, advising the skinning of a portion
of the skull and then burning the bone with an instrument
at white heat, and quite a controversy took place as to whether
the implement used should be of gold, silver, copper, iron, or
of the concentration of the sun's rays with a burning glass.
This cure by cauterization was so highly thought of that the
Academy of Surgery in Paris distinguished with their highest
honors Baron Percy for his work on the subject.

The doctors of to-day are just as much at variance as to
the medicines to be employed, and very rarely effect permanent cures. They fail to see that the disease is a nervous one,
intimately connected with the genital system; and since I
have commenced treating it from this standpoint, with purely

nervine and hygienic prescriptions, I have never met with a total failure. I can assure all troubled with this dreadful disease, that there is a remedy. I have it, and if they would be cured let them apply to me. I have repudiated all superstitions, all cruel methods of treatment, and base my management of the complaint upon that system which I have so thoroughly tested and proved in all cases of nervous excitement or depression arising from hereditary or actual sexual excesses. I lay it down that epilepsy is no longer a cause of locking up patients in a lunatic asylum, or treating them like maniacs or idiots; their complaint can be reached, can be cured by proper treatment, and I have thus cured hundreds who had been given up as confirmed epileptics, only fitted for hospitals for incurables.

The whole fact, in a nutshell, is, that epilepsy is not a disease, existing by itself, but a violent manifestation of derangements of the nervous system, which gives rise to a definite, inseparate condition. Remove the cause, establish nervous health and vigor, and, the cause no longer existing, the effects must cease. This is the key-note to my treatment.

Medical men, as a rule, overlook the sexual question in treating of epilepsy, when in fact it is the foundation of the whole matter; onanism or excess produce it; marriage frequently cures it; numerous cases have occurred from congenital phimosis, and a removal of the prepuce has cured the patient when every other remedy had proved useless.

There are other mental maladies which are sometimes produced by sexual abuse or excess, but as they are of a rarer nature, and have to be treated as a positive insanity, it would be out of place to treat of them in a popular work like the present, except by way of general warning.

CHAPTER XXIII.

OF BRIGHT'S DISEASE AS CAUSED BY EXCESS.

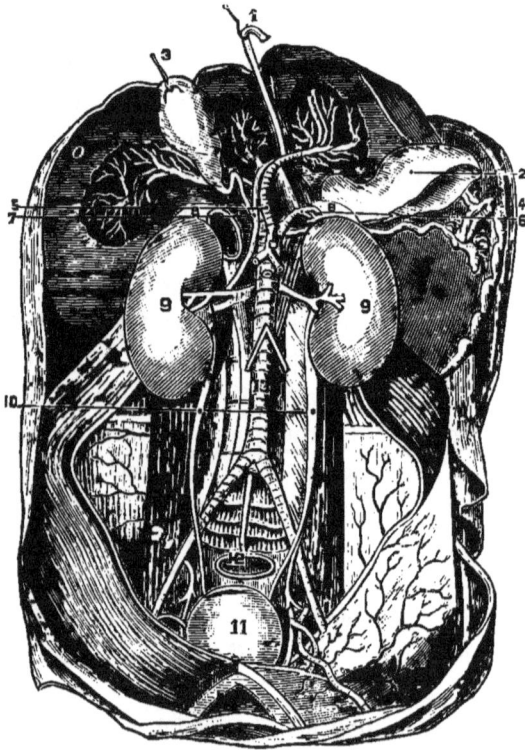

There is one disease, unfortunately very common, and, usually, when neglected in its earlier stages, rapidly fatal, to which I have directed much attention, and which, though not absolutely created by youthful errors or mature excesses of a sexual character, is frequently induced by them, and which is more likely to result from exposure to damp or cold when the body is already weakened by a drainage of its more precious juices. This is what is usually known as Bright's Disease—an affection of the kidneys, which can readily be discovered from a careful examination of the urine, and which is so rapidly aggravated by a neglect of the earlier symptoms that the second and third stages are reached before medical aid is called in to arrest its ravages. When once the urethral passage is inflamed, whether from manual pollution, gonorrheal poisoning or the too profuse a use of cantharides and cubebs, the slightest exposure to cold is liable to bring on catarrhal nephritis, as physicians term the earlier stage of inflammation of the kidneys, and which, if not immediately and properly treated, will rapidly degenerate into Bright's disease, which may be divided into three stages—the inflammatory form, the waxy form, and the gouty form. The first form may be subdivided into—inflammation—fatty transformation and atrophy, or a wasting away of the organ. These are followed by degeneration, changes in the tubes, and a positive destruction of the kidneys, with degenerative enlargements of the important glands which connect these organs with the outlet for the secretions, which must end fatally.

The waxy form is generally the result of syphilitic taint, and will, therefore, be treated of in my work on venereal diseases. Gouty kidney occurs more frequently where sexual excesses have been accompanied by heavy drinking, and drunkenness itself, even without genital abuse, is a very common cause of this class of renal disease.

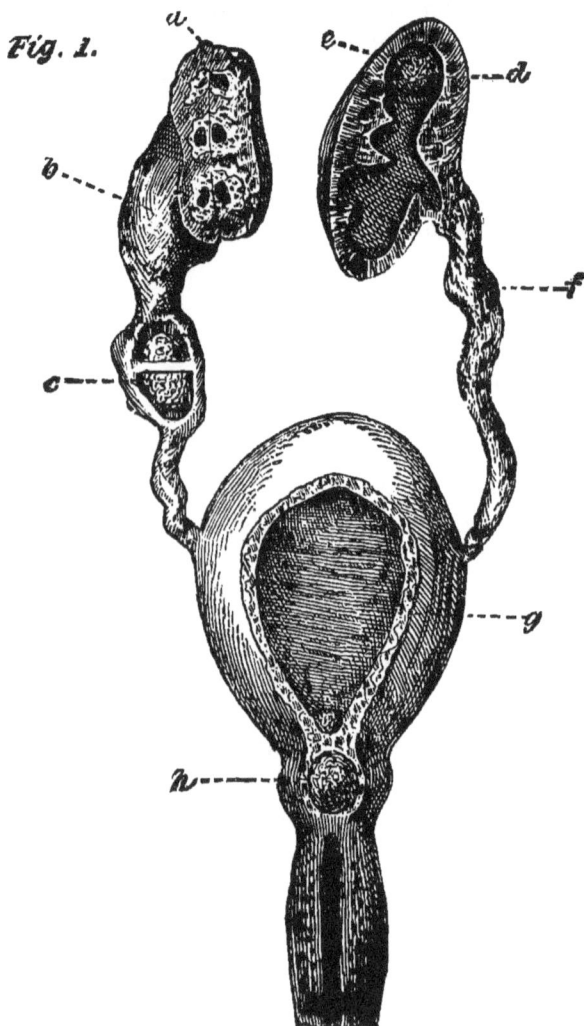

Fig. 1.

The exciting cause of the inflammatory and most usual form of this disease is exposure to cold and wet, especially after exhaustive sensual pleasure. Especially does the wasting away follow the common nostrums prescribed by ignorant pretenders to medicine, who, in the slightest cases, drench their patients with copaiba, cubebs, oil of turpentine, and, for temporary impotence, with cantharides. When once the presence of kidney disease is suspected no time should be lost, a day, an hour, may cause months of trouble.' Prompt and proper action is imperative, and I have saved thousands by taking the disease in time, while those who have succumbed have had themselves to blame for not having consulted me until the second stage, or perhaps the third, was reached, and then no human help could prevent the catastrophe. Avoid drink, use simple diet—farina, milk, beef tea, follow implicitly my directions, and I have no fear of the result, if you are in time. If you put it off I defy the world to save you.

The abuse of the sexual organs, both in the male and female, frequently leads to hypochondriasis, which, in its earlier stages, if not insanity, is so near to it that, unless treated vigorously and at once, it will certainly degenerate into melancholy madness. Its earliest development, as a result of masturbation, is usually accompanied by stomach pains and stubborn fits of indigestion. Schroeder Van der Kolk has graphically described mental disorder arising from self-pollution. His words are :

"If one perceives in a young man a certain degree of shyness, an evasive and cast-down look, a dull, irresolute character, which are soon accompanied by a stupidity and confusion of head and weakness of memory, this worst of all vices is to be predicated. In addition to this, there is an incon-

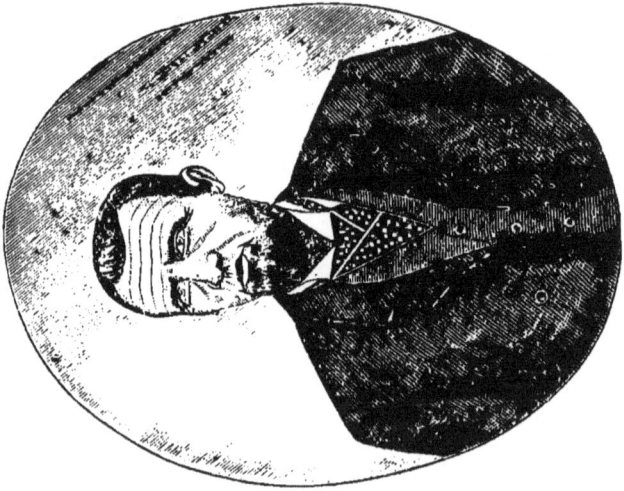

stancy of character and inconsistency of demeanor according as the unhappy tendency is indulged in without restraint." Timidity is another characteristic. The victim of the vice imagines that every man is noticing him; at times fanatical notions and self-accusations follow, and the friendly physician is no longer in doubt. The physical condition is unmistakable, the circulation becomes irregular, the hands are fishy, cold yet perspiring, clammy and unpleasant to the touch, the neck and the back of the head are hot. Biting of the nails, scratching of the fingers, the presence of hang nails, and sluggish movement of the bowels, are also signs. The dulness of look is quite characteristic of the disease, and this increases until the diminution of the intellectual power finally passes into dementia or idiocy.

When a young man has placed before him the results of his secret pleasures thus plainly, when he knows that physical sickness, mental debility and intellectual extinction follow in their train, he certainly will abandon the habit; but, unfortunately, a false modesty too frequently prevents a parent or a friend from pointing out these things, and books like the present do not fall into his hands.

I have not yet gone through one-half of the diseases which arise from masturbation, and which accompany that weakening of the powers which results from a constant drain upon the genital forces. Nature tries all she can to supply the demand, and while she is bound a bond-slave to secret lusts, and has to supply fluid to be wasted, she is compelled to neglect other parts of the body, and they are left a prey to disease and destruction. No amount of labor, no exposure to the influences of the changing seasons, no hardships in the way of coarse food, no continued work with any portion of

the frame enervates the body and leaves it a prey to diseases
of all kinds, as too frequent emissions of semen, especially
when such expulsions are caused by self-friction ; the spasms
which ensue bring on all the infirmities of old age, loosen
the teeth, makes the hair fall off, give palsied tremulousness
to the limbs, a haggard thinness to the cheeks, a livid and
unhealthy paleness to the complexion, a want of sensitiveness
to the tympanum of the ear, to the retina of the eye, the
hearing becomes hard, the optic nerve refuses to carry the
sense of external objects to the brain ; and, in fact, one year's
experience in masturbation is equal to ten of hard labor, and
the youth of twenty has all the weaknesses of the decrepit
old man of three score years and ten, without his moral force
of character to make up for the loss of physical power.
Among all the list of chronic diseases incidental to humanity,
I do not know one which may not be brought on by onanism.
It is the forerunner of physical decay ; the harbinger of
mania and idiocy ; the parent of epilepsy ; the sowing of the
seeds of consumption ; the exciting agent for piles ; the accessory to Bright's various terrible diseases of the kidneys ;
the blinder of the eye ; the stopper of the ear ; the fruitful
source of scorbutic humor, itching, scurvy and determined
scrofula ; the handmaid to dementia ; the goader to madness ;
the chamberlain to death.   The sexton's spade never more
surely dug a grave for youth and beauty than does the sacri-
legious hand which is laid with lustful grasp upon the ark of
manhood and the fruit-tree of the world's increase.   It carries
with it the curse of God, and every masturbator has the indeli-
ble mark somewhere on his body or in his brain as surely and
as firmly placed as was the sign of Almighty anger on the
first murderer, Cain.   Every onanist is a moral suicide, and

it would be better for himself and society if he straightened a halter or stopped a Derringer ball.

But do not let me be too harsh ; Nature, though bound to revenge every outrage upon her, is not tyrannical. Stop your hand, cease the practice and seek a cure. For every disease she, in her bounteous storehouse, has concealed a remedy. Those who seek diligently shall find ; and in the SAMARITAN NERVINE has been discovered a searching potency which will penetrate the blood, enter into the grand system of nerves, and renew the drooping power. It will give to the system that strength of which the seminal drain has deprived it, and by removing the cause cure the consequences, whether they be found in the liver, the kidneys, the brain, or the procreative organs. The only thing is, take it in time, before the recuperative power of nature, thus assisted, has absolutely destroyed tissues necessary for life. It can strengthen, it can remove obstructions, it can heal, but it cannot create. If the organs are still intact, I will guarantee a cure ; if absolute and positive destruction of tissues has taken place, no power on earth, no medicine ever made, can replace them. Come to me, I will be honest with you, and if the last die has been thrown, the last chance gone by, I will tell you so, and by the Nervine, and other remedies, prolong life and make existence a pleasure instead of a burden. I have made the barren fruitful, raised those whose passions had dribbled away in a long and unnoticed flood of life's richest products ;— have restored the failing eyesight, steadied the shaking limb, put flesh upon the attenuated frame, and arrested intellectual decay ; have made useful members of society those who, in a few months, would have been driveling idiots, and all from the body-destroying, soul-killing vice of masturbation ; I have taken patients whose spermatic juices were reduced to a mere watery exudation, emitted without pleasure, even without consciousness of its loss, except by the deadly effects upon the system, and have cured them. I have undertaken cases where the urine was filled with albumen, and the kidneys were rapidly approaching the destructive stage, and they are now hale, hearty men. I have had under my care the trembling, nervous epileptic, who has, at a moment's notice, fallen to earth like a log, and remained unconscious for hours, and have removed the epileptic tendency so that there has been no return. I have arrested the departing intellect as it was bidding farewell to the brain, and leaving hopeless idiocy traced in unmistakable lines upon the face of the masturbator; and the man and woman live to-day in their right senses, attending to their daily business, and I have yet to register my first failure where the disease has been taken in time. Do not delay, then, but come at once ; or, if you cannot come, send a detailed account of your symptoms, and the causes. You can place implicit confidence in me ; I will keep your secret sacred, and will cure you.

Young man, does your eye fail, is your hearing heavy, have you pains in the back of your head and a heaviness over your eyes ? Do the last drops of urine feel sticky or oily between the fingers, have you a troublesome cough, does the scrotum hang lower than it should do ? Does the effort made by going to stool cause an unusual moisture to ooze from the penis, have you pains across the small of the back, are you obliged to leap from bed with sudden cramps in the foot or leg, is your sleep disturbed by lascivious dreams, have you a singing sound in the ears ? Take either of these symptoms as a warning if you have ever outraged nature, tampered with your manly powers

or given way to secret lust. Do not delay; to-morrow may
be too late. Consult me, personally or by letter, at once. I
will tell you what is the matter and guarantee a cure. Why
will you die, or drag out an existence of fear and trembling ?
The Samaritan Nervine was made for you. It will make you
sound. If, in addition to any of these symptoms, or in place
of them, you suffer from an impure connexion, get my book
on disorders arising from promiscuous intercourse, and you
find every degree and kind described, explained, and the
remedy pointed out. No man is wise at all hours, said the
philosopher, and you may have had your weak moment and
fallen a victim to the pestilence which haunts the home of
debauch and lust. To err is human, to forgive divine ; and to
find a remedy for the consequences of error, the duty of the
physician.

Unfortunately for the young, and for the middle aged too,
for that matter, it is not by infection alone that the life-giving
organs are ruined, the constitution destroyed, and life itself
placed in jeopardy. Over the very sunshine of existence
hangs a black cloud. With the uncertainty of life is mingled
the dark mystery of death ! While on the one hand we catch
the welcome sound of a new breath of life that tells of an addition to our species, on the other we shudder as we hear the
rushing wings of the Destroying Angel ! The mighty voice of
the Great Influence which rules the Universe has pronounced
our fate ; the dread fiat has gone forth, and every mortal man
is doomed to die ! But, though we cannot prevent, can we
postpone death ? The question is momentous, even if it con-
cern the prolongation of life but by a single hour, inasmuch
as every instinct prompts us to fight the boldest battle we can
for this glorious boon of existence. The promptings of in-

stinct are but the spontaneous voices of nature, and it is our
duty to obey. But there still remains the question, *can* death
be postponed by a single hour ?

The Fell Destroyer makes his first approaches in many
forms, but none are more favored by him than that of a deadly
foe now preying upon the very vitals of modern society.
What is this foe ? There are few among us who have not
been or are now to some extent its victims. Would the reader
know if he, too, is under the ban of this frightful scourge ?

Let him ask himself whether he has trifled with his manhood ; whether he has sapped his vital power by draining the
system of its choicest fluids ? Has he allowed secret lusts to
bear him beyond the barriers of virtue ? Let the young
woman just budding into maturity ask whether she has kept
her virgin vessel from rifling hands ; whether she has not run
the risk of entailing upon her future some of those painful
diseases which make female life a burden ? How few can
say they have never sinned ; and if they have, ever so little,
they may have incipient disease which, if neglected, time will
ripen into suffering, barrenness, impotence, perhaps lunacy
and death.

Watch your health carefully, mark how you sleep, and
whether you feel uneasy in the morning. Have you experienced any of the following symptoms ?

There are pains about the chest and sides, and sometimes
in the back. The mouth has a bad taste, especially in the
morning ; and there are feelings of dullness and drowsiness.
The appetite is poor, a sort of sticky slime collects about the
teeth, there is a feeling as of a heavy load on the stomach,
and sometimes a faint, all-gone sensation at the pit of the
stomach, which food does not satisfy. The eyes are sunken,

the hands and feet become cold and clammy. After a while a cough sets in, at first dry, but attended in the course of a few months with expectoration of a greenish color. The sufferer feels constantly tired, and sleep seems to afford him no rest. Nervousness, irritability, and evil forebodings follow. When rising suddenly there is a giddiness, a sort of whirling sensation in the head. The bowels become costive ; the skin is dry and hot at times ; the blood becomes thick and stagnant ; the whites of the eyes are tinged with yellow ; the urine is scanty and high colored, depositing a sediment after standing. There is frequently a spitting up of the food—at times with a sour taste and at others with a sweetish taste. This is often attended with palpitation of the heart or impaired vision, with spots before the eyes, accompanied by great prostration and weakness. All of these symptoms are in turn present.

CHAPTER XXIV.

A WONDERFUL CURE IN ENGLAND.

Some of our most celebrated medical men go so far as to say that more than two-thirds of our total population between fourteen and twenty-eight are either directly or indirectly suffering from the consequences of concealed and frequently unsuspected weakness of the generative organs, while half the elder balance are, in some way, slaves to either the too profuse use of these organs or the neglect of them, for conti-.nence has its martyrs as well as excess. Many mistake the.

nature of their malady, and too many medical men ignore its
origin, but its true name is involuntary loss of semen, and
the only certain remedy yet discovered, one proved efficacious
after a thousand trials, is the Samaritan Nervine; a medicine
which has won in both hemispheres a confidence which could
only be founded on universal success and on its radical
virtues.

I could fill volumes with letters of thankfulness, with
unsolicited testimonials to the miraculous powers of the
Nervine, letters from scholars and from the illiterate, testimonials from the wealthy and the poor, thanks from the
palace and the hut. Here is one which I have received from
across the Atlantic, for my Samaritan Nervine is known as
well on the banks of the Thames as on the mighty waters of
the Big Muddy. This letter is of double force, as it was not
written to me but to an intimate friend of the sufferer, and
from that friend I got it :

"DEAR NED—

"You will be surprised at receiving a letter from me, but,
thank God, I am pleased to say I am getting better every day.
I shall be so glad to breathe the fresh air again. It has
seemed a dreadful long time to be in bed. You know I was
taken to the hospital last April to be treated for Bright's
disease of the kidneys. Well, on the 31st of July they tapped
me and took away 304 ounces of water. The same thing
was done again on the 18th September and 408 ounces of
water obtained. On the 9th October I was discharged from
the hospital as incurable. In January this year (the 20th)
was again tapped at home and 300 ounces of water taken
away. The St. Bartholomew's Hospital in London refused
me admission as a hopeless case, and the St. Bartholomew's

Hospital, Chatham, also refused me, as being the worst case they had seen for years, and two local doctors gave me up as hopeless. When I came from the hospital it took three to put me to bed. My clothes had to be cut off. I was an object of misery and despair. After the hospitals had refused me, and doctors given me up, I was persuaded to try a bottle of Dr. Richmond's Samaritan Nervine, an American remedy, made by a medical man of great renown, who lives on the borders of the great Missouri River. Utterly hopeless, I thought at any rate a trial could do no harm. It acted like magic; the improvement was immediate. After seven weeks I could get down stairs and even attend a little to my business, the pains in the small of the back were gone, there was no longer a muciiaginous discharge from the urethra. A few more bottles and I shall be well. Could I only have crossed the Atlantic and paid that wonderful doctor a visit I feel certain that my recovery would have been still more accelerated. I wish I had tried it earlier, before I ruined myself with doctors' bills. When at the hospital I had no appetite, and now it would do you good to see how I eat. After taking the Nervine everything goes down with a relish. If you have any friends suffering, let them, for God's sake, know how I was and how I am,

> "*For I would trumpet all around*
> *The wondrous med'cine I have found.*

"I am, your affectionate friend,
"JOHN JAMES RATHBORNE.
"*No. —— Smith street, Chelsea, England.*"

One of the most eminent of our Western surgeons says: Kidney disease is probably, next to consumption. the commonest cause of death among adults in this climate. You have had a recent and mysterious attack of asthma, pains in the back and around the loins, severe headaches, dizziness, inflamed eyes, a coated tongue and a dry mouth, loss of appetite, chilly sensation (the stomach never is in order when the kidneys or liver are deranged), dryness of the skin, nervousness, night sweats, muscular debility, despondency, a tired feeling (especially at night), puffing or bloating under the eyes, and your muscular system seems utterly helpless. Dr. Roberts, of England; Professor Thompson, of New York, and other celebrated authorities tell us that all these symptoms are sure indications of Bright's disease! With some patients the disease runs slowly and for years. With others it comes as a thief in the night. This fact is an alarming one, and starts the inquiry, What can be done?

This book tells you what can be done. It points out the way to life, health and happiness. Why will you die? when the Samaritan Nervine is ready at hand to relieve and save you. It may have been produced by sexual excess, it may be the result of solitary habits. The terrible sin and crime of drunkenness may have brought it on. A bad cold, a damp bed, wet feet, a malarious climate, may be to blame. No matter, the cure covers all, and, if taken in time, I have no hisitation in saying that death from Bright's disease is absolutely impossible.

Thus, within the limits of a moderate-sized book, I have endeavored to show what Manhood and Womanhood are, what pleasures they may enjoy, what dangers are around them, and I feel certain that if this work be carefully read, thought over and obeyed, it will save thousands from prolonged misery and shortened lives.

I have but one more duty to perform, and then my task is ended, and the work which contains the experience of years ready to go on its mission of usefulness to humanity. This is to glance at the treatment of spermatorrhea and its kindred complaints, such as leucorrhea in females, etc. Aperients and tonics are generally found of much benefit, as are chalybeates and sudorifics, with such drugs as have an anti-aphrodisiac and anti-spasmodic quality. Narcotics and sedatives are absolutely necessary in allaying the more painful and unpleasant symptoms; opium, belladonna, hyoscyamum, morphia and bromide of potassia are all in turn useful, either combined or in a separate form. These remedies, when judiciously employed, prevent the nocturnal emissions; but, as they are apt to cause constipation of the bowels, they must be varied with mild aperients. These facts have been carefully studied in the concoction of the Samaritan Nervine, and only such vegetable substances have been used in its preparation as are free from the dangers attendant upon opiates, and no fear of the irregularity of bowels need prevent the most delicately constituted patient from taking it.

Of course a disease which has so many variations and such wonderful changes in its form of attack requires a variety of remedies, according to the seat and nature of the affection. Thus, amnerosis, deafness, loss of taste, smell or touch, partial or general convulsions, spasms, etc., will call for their apposite medicines, each differing from the other.

Some drugs have an active and immediate effect upon the genital organs; such as phosphorus, nux vomica, strychnine, copaiba, cubebs, buchu, the turpentines, cantharides, ergot, and a few others, but these require excessive care in their exhibition, or dangers greater than those they cure will result from their use. Used without proper judgment they do incalculable injury, even totally destroying the virile power and causing death. A rapid cure of spermatorrhœa, with functional disturbance of the nervous centres, is absolutely impracticable, and would never be promised by any but the most arrogant quack. Time, in these diseases, is the physician's handmaid, and must assist in restoring the brain and spinal marrow to a normal condition. This once done, the sexual derangement demands attention, and the generative weakness will more rapidly disappear. The great danger lies in the lesions of the brain and spinal cord, and not in the genital apparatus. When the disease is merely a local disturbance of the organs of generation, owing to excessive irritation, the disease is readily cured. An ordinary case can be remedied in from six to nine months, but in cases of several years' standing, from twelve to eighteen months will be found necessary. All vaunted and reported rapid cures are deceptive. After a few weeks' treatment stimulants are administered ; a feeble shadow of manhood is produced, only, when the temporary excitement is over, to leave the deceived patient worse than he was before.

When inflammatory symptoms are present in the seminal vessels, or in the ejaculatories and other ducts, local applications will be found necessary in addition to the remedies prescribed for internal use. Mild injections, either for urethra or vagina, are frequently very efficacious, of which acetate of lead forms the base and water the medium, sometimes mixed with pulverized opium. In other cases more powerful injections, such as nitrate of silver, may be found necessary. External applications, too, I frequently use, and have found wonderful effects from the simple exhibition of crushed ice, or ice water. In constitutions thoroughly broken down from excess or age it will not do to continue these cold applications too long, as gangrene may be induced and life sacrificed, so that it is only under the care of the doctor that these means should be resorted to.

Galvanism, or some other form of electricity, I have found of immense value, but it would be a waste of time to explain the manner of its application, as it must be used under my immediate attention.

Diet is another great desideratum, and it is time and money thrown away if the patient, during treatment, indulges in spiced foods, indigestible pastries, alcoholic stimulants, even such as coffee or beer. Tobacco has been by some medical men praised as almost a remedy by itself, but my experience is to the direct contrary; and in every form in which it may be used I have found it retard the cure and intensify the symptoms.

No feather beds, or fleecy over-warm coverings, can be permitted; they force the disease as hotbeds do plants, and I would not undertake a case at all unless the patient promised to forego them.

Two things, let it be remembered, are imperatively necessary to insure a cure. First, time—there is no hurrying Nature; she is slowly destroyed, and will not, cannot, be rapidly recuperated;—and then, implicit obedience to the orders of the doctor. He knows what he is doing, and will lay down no rules which are not for the patient's welfare.

Obey the one and take the other, and I will guarantee a perfect cure—a permanent release from slavery ten times worse than death. The Samaritan Nervine has a more powerful effect, ten times over, when my directions are rigidly adhered to.

To those who care to study the secrets of human nature, or to those unhappy sufferers from infection who need advice, I recommend a perusal of my new and exhaustive work on the History, Description and Methods of Cure of Syphilis and Other Infectious Diseases of the Genital Organs and the Diseases Arising From Them, which is now in the press, and will immediately be issued.